EXAMPLES OF EARLY ENGLISH POTTERY

No. 404, page 109.

EXAMPLES OF
EARLY ENGLISH POTTERY

NAMED, DATED, AND INSCRIBED.

BY

JOHN ELIOT HODGKIN, F.S.A.,

AND

EDITH HODGKIN.

REPUBLISHED
EP PUBLISHING LIMITED
1973

Publishers' Note

Many of the pieces described in this book have changed hands since the Hodgkins first published *Examples of Early English Pottery* in a limited edition of 550 copies in 1891.

However, since most of these pieces belonged to the great early collectors, who were responsible for preserving so much of the English earthenware tradition, their current whereabouts can often be traced from the relevant sale catalogues of such firms as Sotheby's and Christie's.

In addition many of the pieces are now to be found in the collections of museums, both in the United Kingdom and overseas.

ISBN 0 85409 900 X

Please address all enquiries to EP Publishing Ltd.
(address as above)

Reprinted in Great Britain by
The Scolar Press Limited, Menston, Yorkshire

A LIST

OF THE

Possessors of Early English Pottery

MENTIONED IN THIS WORK.

Name.	*Abbreviation.*
Baines, F.	*F. Ba.*
Biddell, M.	*M. B.*
Blackmore, Dr.	*Dr. B.*
Bodenham, F.	*F. B.*
Boynton, T.	*T. B.*
Bruce, J.	*J. B.*
Clarke, A. E.	*A. E. C.*
Clements, W.	*W. C.*
De L'Isle and Dudley, The Right Hon. Lord	*Lord de L.*
Doel, —	*— D.*
Edkins, W. (the late)	*The late W. E.*
Evans, Dr. J.	*Dr. J. E.*
Fisher, R. (the late)	*The late R. F.*
Ford, J. W.	*J. W. F.*
Fraser, Col.	*Col. F.*
Griffiths, H.	*H. G.*
Hawkins, J.	*J. Ha.*
Hext, Miss F. M.	*F. M. H.*
Hodgkin, Edith	*E. H.*
Hodgkin, John Eliot	*J. E. H.*
Hodgkin, John	*J. H.*
Institute, Mechanics', Hanley	*M. I. H.*
,, Pottery Mechanics', Shelton	*P. M. I.*
,, Wedgwood, Burslem	*W. I. B.*
Jull, Miss	*E. J.*
Jull, W.	*W. J.*
Kidd, Samuel	*S. K.*
Moffatt, H. C.	*H. C. M.*
Montgomery, Dr.	*Dr. M.*
Moor, Capt.	*Capt. M.*
Mount Edgcumbe, The Right Hon. the Earl of	*Earl Mt. E.*

LIST OF POSSESSORS.

NAME.	*ABBREVIATION.*
MUSEUMS:—	
BEDFORD	*BED. MUS.*
BRITISH	*B. MUS.*
DUBLIN	*D. MUS.*
GUILDHALL	*G. MUS.*
HANLEY	*H. MUS.*
LIVERPOOL (MAYER)	*L. MUS.*
MAIDSTONE	*M. MUS.*
NORWICH	*N. MUS.*
NOTTINGHAM CASTLE	*N. C. MUS.*
PRACTICAL GEOLOGY	*M. P. G.*
SALFORD	*SA. MUS.*
SALISBURY	*S. MUS.*
SOUTH KENSINGTON	*S. K. MUS.*
TAUNTON	*T. MUS.*
WESTON PARK, SHEFFIELD	*W. P. S. MUS.*
YORK	*Y. MUS.*
NORRIS, DR. HUGH	*DR. H. N.*
PICTHALL, MRS.	*MRS. P.*
PITT-RIVERS, GEN.	*GEN. P. R.*
POLEY, MRS. WELLER	*MRS. W. P.*
POTTS, F.	*F. P.*
PYCROFT, G.	*G. P.*
SACKVILLE, THE RIGHT HON. LORD	*LORD S.*
SLATER, G.	*G. S.*
SODEN-SMITH, R. H. (THE LATE)	*THE LATE R. H. S.-S.*
SMITH, W. (THE LATE)	*THE LATE W. S.*
SOLON, L. M.	*L. M. S.*
STANSBY, J.	*J. S. S.*
STENNING, G.	*G. ST.*
SWANN, J. S.	*J. S.*
TRACY, MRS.	*MRS. T.*
TOPLIS, J. (THE LATE)	*THE LATE J. T.*
WARNE, C. H.	*C. H. W.*
WESTWOOD, PROF.	*PROF. W.*
WILLETT, H.	*H. W.*
WIMBORNE, THE RIGHT HON. LORD	*LORD W.*

INTRODUCTION

Weilcom my Freinds

A RAPID advance in wealth, luxury, and leisure, in any country, is for the most part followed by an increased thirst for the investigation of its early history, for more exhaustive enquiry, on the one hand, into the development of its external and internal growth, and of its prosperity, laws, language, poetry and literature ; and on the other, into the progress made from the most ancient times in its industrial and decorative arts. The former class of researches, dealing as it does with questions which touch the very life and soul of the nation, naturally attracts attention at an earlier period than the latter ; and in the case of our own country, many points in connection with the history of its art have only recently been made the subject of any searching investigation, and others remain still unelucidated. Thus it is that until within the last twenty or thirty years any systematic classification and identification of the various fabriques of our national ceramic industry were unknown, and that to the labours of antiquaries still amongst us, or to those who have but recently passed away, we owe most of our knowledge on this interesting subject.

In the pages of Jewitt, Chaffers, Solon, and Professor Church, the student who is anxious to make himself acquainted with the forms of such earthen vessels as our forefathers were familiar with, and the collector who desires to acquire such a knowledge of the appearance of the various kinds of early pottery which have survived to our day as will enable him to judge discreetly the pieces he may meet with, will each find a large amount of highly interesting and necessary information, so digested, in the case of the two last-mentioned works, as to afford ready means of verification. And not only so, but M. Solon, treating the subject largely from an artistic, and Professor Church from a scientific point of view, alike inspire in the minds of their readers, by the easy and seductive way in which their respective monographs are handled, enthusiasm, curiosity, thirst to possess, desire for further knowledge—in short, just those emotions which are likely to change the easy-going dilettante possessor of a small number of ill-assorted specimens into an ardent, intelligent, and eclectic collector.

It may reasonably then be asked what excuse can be found for still another work treating of Early English Pottery, when the ground has been so fully covered by the works already mentioned. The reply which the authors have to offer is, that the present work is designed to supplement its predecessors, by bringing before the view of its readers (1) accurate representations of a large number of objects of which, as a rule, no illustration has yet been made public; and (2) a list as nearly complete as may be of all the pieces of the selected kinds of Early English Pottery which tell us anything about themselves, which say *when they were made or where, or by whom or for whom, or for what purpose*, thus standing out distinctly from the mass of specimens which on all these points are *dumb*. There is in our opinion much to be gained by such a catalogue. In the case of the two most important subdivisions of our list, *The Slip-Decorated Ware*, and the *Delft or Faïence*, the finest and most representative specimens are almost always the "*speaking*" pieces; and it has seemed to us that the novice will be able to obtain a much sounder basis for his conclusions as to the classification and probable date of any *uninscribed* specimen which he may meet with, from having the opportunity here afforded of comparison with a piece perhaps very similar in form, colour, or decoration, which carries its own evidence as to date and fabrique; whilst the expert and well-trained collector will, on the other hand, look, as we hope, with approval upon an enumeration hitherto quite beyond his reach of all the readily accessible specimens of this class.

In furtherance of these objects, we have—at considerable trouble, as may be understood—obtained, where practicable and desirable, facsimiles of the inscriptions on those pieces which we have not engraved, since much may be learned by analogy and comparison where uncertainty arises as to the approximate date, or even as to the original *provenance* of a specimen bearing no inscription. A careful examination of the letters and figures reproduced will indicate how closely their several types indicate distinct fabriques, and thus afford a useful means of discrimination.

It may be mentioned in passing that it was at the outset intended to compose these inscriptions with movable characters, specially prepared for the various styles of letter, somewhat after the fashion of the edition of the Mediceo-Laurentian Virgil, printed at Florence in the year 1741; or, to cite a more familiar instance, after that of Baber's edition of the Codex Alexandrinus (1816-27). For this purpose a number of alphabets were made, so that the effect could be fairly judged, but the result was not altogether satisfactory, and it was then decided that, as far as was practicable, each inscription should be accurately copied by hand, and a photo-relief block obtained therefrom. The increased accuracy thus gained has of course greatly augmented our labour, and has necessarily caused delay in the production of the volume.

It must not be for a moment supposed that our scheme covers the whole area of English Ceramics. In the first place, as will be self-evident to the expert, it *entirely excludes Porcelain* of every kind, dealing only with those opaque and less highly vitrified wares properly called *Pottery*. In the second, it excludes all the later forms of English pottery, such as Wedgwood, Leeds, and other recent earthenware. These wares were the outcome of a rapidly changing civilisation, and were produced in large factories with all the appliances for turning out work in large quantities; and although, as in the case of Wedgwood, a high order of culture and refinement, and great technical skill, were often called into requisition, their products are entirely outside our range. We have to do with specimens produced, in some cases, in isolated little potteries, the very place and name of which has not reached us, and in others, in factories of the old school, now deserted and in ruins, of which, with the exception of that at Fulham, it may be said, that having filled their place in their country's history, they died and left absolutely no successors. They owed their being largely to the dearness of metal wares, and to the comparative lack of those glass vessels of all kinds now accessible (too often, alas! from foreign sources) to the very poorest folks in the land.

Almost every piece described has its own separate history and meaning; in some few cases it formed a portion of a set, but for the most part each specimen carries its own distinctive credentials.

We have decided without difficulty which of the old wares to omit from our category. We exclude not only ancient British, Roman, and Anglo-Saxon, but also that highly important branch of English Ceramics, the encaustic tiles, intensely interesting though they are from their beauty and historical associations. These have already been thoroughly described and magnificently illustrated.

And even if it were not so, they are inadmissible from the fact that they were, to a large extent, produced from moulds, and their legends and devices thus indefinitely multiplied.

In this connection it seems well to note that we have refused admission to *all those pieces in which the whole inscription is produced from a mould*, as well as to all such as merely bear the name or initials of a Sovereign; these latter occur in considerable numbers among the existing specimens of English Delft, but as they were doubtless made for general sale, we have had reluctantly, for they are often quaint beyond belief, to show them the door.

It is after mediæval days that our task begins, and the following list roughly sets forth the principal varieties of English Pottery occurring since the beginning of the sixteenth century. An asterisk indicates a variety which it has been attempted to deal with:—

(I.) Green-Glazed Buff Ware.
(II.) Brown-Glazed Red Ware.*
(III.) Elers' Red Ware (1690).

(IV.) Dwight's Fulham Stoneware (1671).
(V.) Slip-Decorated Ware.*
(VI.) Lambeth, Bristol, Liverpool, and other Delft Wares.*
(VII.) White Salt-Glazed Stoneware.*
(VIII.) Fulham Brown Stoneware.*
(IX.) Nottingham and Allied Stonewares.*
(X.) Agate, Marble, and Combed Wares.
(XI.) Tortoiseshell Ware.
(XII.) Lambeth Stoneware.*
(XIII.) Black Basaltes Ware.
(XIV.) White and Cream-Coloured Earthenwares.
(XV.) Jasper Ware.

etc. etc. etc.

(I.) The *Green-glazed Ware*, with a buff body, which heads the list, is called Tudor ware; we would willingly have described and reproduced any specimens of this Pottery which bear inscribed names, dates, or legends, but the only pieces of this character with which we are acquainted have the letters *moulded* in relief—*e.g.*, tiles in B.M. with initials E.R., and a fragment in J.E.H.'s own collection of probably still earlier date, decorated with the Tudor Rose and initials H. (R.).

(II.) The simple *Brown-glazed Red Ware* affords us very few named, dated, or inscribed specimens, but these are all the more interesting, not only by reason of their rarity, but also from the widely spread use of this thoroughly domestic Pottery, of which thousands of fragments have turned up in broken condition. Illustrations of the "tygs" of this ware will be found in almost all the works cited.

The tyg was, before the introduction first of separate mugs, and subsequently of glasses, the cup common to all the guests at convivial gatherings, and was furnished on all sides with suitable handles (very odd-looking to the modern eye), which probably indicated the portion of the cup from which each *convive* was to drink. These vessels, and others of the same body and glaze, must, from the conditions of their employment, have been made in countless thousands, and a certain not inconsiderable proportion doubtless bore dates and inscriptions; yet it will be observed that only a very small number of such have come under our notice. *Sgrafiato* forms an offshoot of this ware.

It is to our great regret that no specimens of the next ware, that of *Elers* (No. III.), are to be found in our catalogue. This Pottery is among the most interesting in the whole series. In spite of the fact that its originators were foreigners, it is one of the most truly national and typical of all the products of English kilns. The paste is of a character differing in its hardness and density from all others, and possessing, in spite of its opacity and dark colour, many of the attributes of porcelain. The treatment of the simple decoration which characterises it is artistic and gratifying, and the aims of the makers were distinctly higher than those of most of their predecessors and successors. But, alas! We have not met with a single instance of date or inscription on any *Elers'* piece other than impressed, either in public or private collections.

(IV.) Of *Dwight's Stoneware* it would be impossible to speak in terms of too high appreciation. His works possess the charm at once of extreme rarity and absolute originality. They are to English Pottery what the productions made at *Oiron* (commonly known as Henri Deux ware) are to the French, and it appears to us that only adverse circumstances stood in the way of a universal appreciation of Dwight's name as the most honourable amongst English potters. The only dated piece of his which has come down to us is the beautiful half-length figure of his infant daughter, in the South Kensington Museum. For a magnificent example of Dwight's work, the reader is referred to the bust of Prince Rupert in the British Museum.

The specimens in this volume which will in all probability attract the most genuine interest are those which fall under the next subdivision.

(V.) *Slip-Decorated Ware.*—Something in them, quaint, bizarre, and to our eyes old-fashioned, arrests the attention, engages the fancy, and at last compels an affection for which perhaps it would be difficult to render a sufficient reason. The collector who has once been bitten with the desire to possess pieces of this ware, will hardly rest until he has by hook or by crook made himself master of many, those of course by preference which bear an inscription or date. It is, to a greater extent than perhaps any other, the *"Old English ware" par excellence*, making few pretensions to beauty, but wholly picturesque, decorated by unlearned potters for patrons often no less illiterate,—relying upon the contrast of rich though simple tints, half-buried beneath a lustrous glaze, rather than upon delicate outlines and graceful decoration, it is still possessed of a charm which, once felt, continues to haunt, and of a power to gladden the ingle-nook or the homely shelf, denied to all the self-sufficient productions of to-day.

It is especially in the *home*, amid simple surroundings and in low rooms half-lit, that this ware best holds its own, for there we are at the same time soothed by the blending of its harmonious and soft yet brilliant reflections, and enlivened by the absolute individuality of its inscriptions. If our spirits flag we are exhorted to BE MERY AND WIS(E), if oppressed by the evil around us, we unite in the heartfelt prayer of the potter, HELP · LORD · FOR · GOOD · AND · GODLY · MEN · DO (FAIL?);—our loyal feelings are stirred by the exhortation to OBEAY THE KING,—our amatory instincts stimulated and put upon a sensible footing by the injunction (no doubt the outcome of a world of experience!) BRISK · BE · TO · THE · MED · YOV · DESIER · AS · HER · LOVE · YOV · MA · REQVIRE,—and finally our gossips and we may cheerfully wind up the day in compliance with the festive suggestion—COM · GOOD · WEMAN · DRINK · OF · THE · BEST · IHON · MY · LADY · AND · ALL · THE · REST. For homely surroundings the ware was created; such it befits, and half its spell is lost when posset-pots, dishes, cradles, puzzle-jugs, and all are crowded together on the white shelves of some greatly receptive yet barely hospitable museum. So few pieces have escaped the ravages of time and ancillary manipulations, that all important and genuine specimens are eagerly sought after at high prices. Modern imitations, however, often of considerable merit, exist in some abundance as pitfalls for the unwary.

This Slip-ware may take rank along with No. VII. (the *White Salt-glazed*

Stoneware) as the most important of the early indigenous English ceramic products. It owed allegiance to no contemporary foreign source, though some have claimed for it a Roman origin, and whatever it possesses of distinctive character is essentially national.

The series of productions which occupy the next place on our list (VI.) are, on the contrary, outspoken imitations of the *faïence* of Holland (well known as Delft), itself again an economical substitute for the Oriental porcelain then as ever highly esteemed in Europe. But although not an entirely new departure, *English Delft* rapidly assumed an interesting character of its own—and this, to some extent, involuntarily.

The Dutch clays were of a soft and friable character when burnt; the English dense and hard, and being less absorbent of the tin enamel to which the white colour of the ware is due, the result was in many cases an approach to the appearance of porcelain even closer than that of the Dutch Delft. This is especially true of the best period of Bristol Delft, whilst in Lambeth Delft there is an indescribable softness in the enamel which only occurs elsewhere, as far as I know, in some kinds of Italian *faenza*. Its occasional change to a pale rose-colour, the result of the thinness of the coating of the enamel over the biscuit, gives it a particular charm. The whole series of English Delft possesses characteristics of great interest. Made by workmen more highly skilled, for a more critical class of customers, it was far more dependent for its effect upon good potting and careful decoration than were the more homely slip-decorated pieces just mentioned.

Oriental suggestion is of course to be expected in a ware which looks back to Oriental porcelain for its inspiration, and three of the pieces which we illustrate (Nos. 314, 325, 351) contain exemplifications of this influence. Some inscriptions, too, have evidently been painted by German workmen (Nos. 310 and 311), and it is well known that in the case of Lambeth Delft, as of early salt-glazed ware, Dutch workmen were originally employed as possessing a skill which our own potters could in the first instance not be expected to supply. An interesting series of *wine-jars* will be found described among the specimens of Lambeth Delft. No satisfactory explanation of the *raison d'être* of these well-known vessels has yet been given; they are too small, it would seem, to have been made for storing wine of a certain vintage, as one might have thought possible from the inscription on No. 300, and if merely intended for serving wine at the tavern, the intention of the date is not very evident. Until the publication of the present volume, the existence of only 41 of these inscribed wine-jars had been recorded; it will be seen that we have been able to bring up the number to 72, only two of this number being undated, and many other specimens are almost certainly in existence. Readers of Champfleury's charming sketch, "Le Violon de Faïence," a work which only an avid collector could have written, in which the connoisseur will recognise as sad and sober verities traits that to the uninitiated must appear to be fantastically overdrawn and cynically exaggerated, will remember that the famous violin had obtained so great a renown in Europe, that a warm discussion arose concerning its nationality, and that an audacious Dutchman had the impertinence to hazard an opinion that the precious object had its birth not in France but in Holland, and communicated his views to the "Faïence Club," only, however, to find his thesis in turn pulverised by a coalition of the very amateurs who had severally claimed this glorious piece for Rouen, for Niederviller, for Nevers, for Marseilles, for Ilettes, and for Sinceny.

Precisely similar difficulties arise in our day in the attribution of our own *faïence*. These tin-enamelled wares were not made in so many different localities in England as in France; yet in many of our public collections, and in some of the works on the subject, there is evidence of want of care in distinguishing between the three principal varieties, and, worse still, a tendency to attribute Dutch pieces to English makers. The task is unquestionably a difficult one, and we make no pretensions to more than an average power of discrimination, fortified by a fairly close acquaintance with the best accredited specimens, and by the comparison of different styles of decoration, but we earnestly hope that but few glaring errors will be found in our analysis. It is almost impossible, in the compass of a few pages, or indeed by any written hints, however carefully indited, to explain to the tyro what we believe to be the distinctive attributes of the glaze, colour, and decoration of these various fabriques; but in deference to the valuable suggestion of Mr. A. W. Franks, we have thought it worth while to append a list of some pieces of Delft, which, *although possessing English inscriptions*, were certainly made in Holland, and in some cases are marked with the monogram of well-known Dutch potters.

These reproductions, which will be found at the end of the volume, teach of course only by the decoration, the difference in glaze and colour being beyond the powers of a written description.

It is interesting to note that English enterprise followed closely on the introduction of the ware by the Dutch, at that time a friendly nation, and that, whilst of the new *faience*, the earliest dated piece of Dutch Delft dates from 1600, we have an example of a distinctly English specimen as early as 1631 (No. 228). But Dutch rivalry in this as in other more important matters ran our countrymen very hard, and divers enactments were made with the intention of prohibiting the importation of the foreign wares. The national production appears to have been on a very extensive scale, and a fair number of specimens, inscribed and otherwise, remain to attest the popularity of this new and decorative ware. Some well-finished specimens of Bristol Delft so closely resemble the Oriental porcelain they were designed to imitate, that without handling them detection is almost impossible. The well-known and coveted tiles manufactured by Sadler and Green, of Liverpool, do not come under our notice, as the beautiful vignettes they bear are the result of transfer *printing*, and not of decoration by hand.

We have already alluded to the *White Salt-glazed Ware* (No. VII.) as eminently national in its origin and characteristics, and it is matter for regret that so few pieces, on which inscriptions of any kind occur, have come under our notice, except those produced in quantities by moulds. The reason for this peculiarity is, however, not far to seek. The beauty of the ware depended rather upon the elegance or quaintness of its form than upon its colour. And where colour was employed it was for the most part either a blue roughly scratched in, or an enamel in imitation of the decoration on Oriental porcelain, and neither of these processes lent themselves very kindly to the employment of inscription. A motto entirely quaint and picturesque in slip-formed capitals would look poor and wiry when simply scratched in cursive letters with a point on the surface of the clay. So much has been so well said in enthusiastic praise by M. Solon, Professor Church, and the late Mr. Soden Smith of this delightful ware, that any expression of opinion on our part would be superfluous; but we cannot forbear the remark that the pieces which bear inscriptions such as we have reproduced afford no conception of the beauty of the un-inscribed pieces, and we earnestly recommend a study of the above-mentioned works, and an inspection of the remarkable assemblage of specimens presented by Lady Charlotte Schreiber to the South Kensington Museum, and of the smaller but representative one on the shelves at the British Museum. Those amateurs who once acquire good pieces of this fascinating and decorative pottery are not likely to be easily checked in their desire to emulate larger collections.

The next ware on our list (No. VIII.), *Fulham Brown Stoneware*, is one which, with the allied productions of *Lambeth and Nottingham* (Nos. XII. and IX.), appeals perhaps with the greatest force to the everyday observer of Old English Pottery. Under these heads are to be classed the countless thousands of "Old Brown Jugs" which, filled with foaming ale, have for more than a century and a half gladdened English hostelries, English homes, and English hearts. Without this familiar fountain of cheerfulness, no picture of an English convivial middle-class meeting of those days was complete The lordly Oriental punch-bowl with the serpentine ribbon of lemon-peel curling on its rim was for the city roysterer of the "Modern Midnight Conversation," but the honest brown jug of Fulham, Lambeth, or perhaps Nottingham ware, for the robust guest of the village ale-house, or the cottage fireside. No vessel forms a more typical adjunct of English social life, and we must not look askance at the various forms of the ware because they do not possess the picturesque contrast of tints or the graceful contours of many other objects which we have to review. The Mug, with its parallel sides, direct offspring of the Tyg, was apparently an earlier form than the wide-mouthed Jug with globular belly, but there seems no reason to doubt that narrow-necked jugs, in imitation of the "Bellarmines" of German origin, were made in considerable numbers in England. It is matter for regret that none of these have as yet been found to bear a date, though we are able to illustrate one with initials. A curious freak of fashion seems to have decreed that an enormous preponderance of Fulham and Lambeth mugs and jugs should have the upper half of their sides coloured dark brown, whilst the rest of the surface retained the natural colour of the clay. This peculiarity, a somewhat remarkable instance of survival, remains to this day in the Doulton and other similar wares; and in the same way the stag-hunts in relief on the Fulham pots of a century and a half ago have come down practically unchanged to our own times.

The *Jackfield* ware, of which a few examples will be found, belongs essentially to the class of Old English Pottery, though its manufacture has survived to comparatively recent times. It appears to be a lineal descendant of the brilliant dark-brown glazed ware, of which Tygs were the earliest exponent, although its surface may have been derived from a somewhat different source.

It possesses a strong idiosyncrasy, and as a contrast to white napery is especially picturesque. It was so popular for a short time that we doubt not that very many inscribed pieces other than those we have recorded are in existence; but as its decoration is not burnt into the glaze, but is effected by means of oil-gilding, many specimens have by use lost their distinguishing features.

Having now indicated the nature of the task which we have set ourselves, we may as well briefly describe the way in which it has been accomplished. Hardly any classified material was ready to our hand. The catalogues of the collections at the Museum of Practical Geology at Jermyn Street, and of the Schreiber collection at South Kensington, are almost the only lists which attempt to furnish any systematic information to the student. A considerable number of specimens have been described, and in some cases illustrated, in the various works treating of Early English Pottery to which we have referred, and in others of the same class. Some of these pieces we have been compelled to admit into our pages just as there mentioned, and without personal scrutiny. We have thought it right, whenever practicable, to inspect the collections in the several museums, and when this could not be conveniently done, to obtain the assistance of the curator—most obligingly rendered—in perfecting the list of those objects which came within our range.

Our next source of information has been found in the well-known private collections of the country; and here again we have gratefully to acknowledge the kindness which has been afforded us by their owners, an obligation which will be hereafter more fully avowed. Finally we have succeeded by means of advertisement, and by the kind offices of friends, in unearthing the records of smaller and less-known stores, often containing perhaps but one single speaking specimen. Thus in various ways we have brought together what may claim to be considered a fully representative catalogue of the inscribed pieces now remaining in the country, at best but a sorry remnant of what it once contained. But we are entirely conscious that scores, possibly hundreds, of such pieces are still buried, often in unappreciative recesses, hidden on forgotten shelves, cumbering dusty cupboards, or, on the other hand, so jealously hoarded that they seldom see the light of day. We shall hope to hear more of some of these as one result of our labours. Much trouble has, we fear, been entailed on our very numerous correspondents by our requirements, as in all cases in which a reproduction was required, a very perfect photograph of the object was indispensable, and in the case of coloured specimens it was essential that the negatives should be produced on *isochromatic* plates, often not to be obtained in country places. Moreover, where no reproduction of the whole specimen was desired, a facsimile of the inscription was generally asked for, and in almost every case most courteously given. Time and pains have been ungrudgingly expended in the attempt to obtain such information on all points as would ensure an accurate description in our pages of each specimen; but we must disclaim entire responsibility for every detail.

Not every possessor of a rare piece has the experience or critical discernment needful for its accurate attribution and description, and his possible errors must consequently remain uncorrected.

The photographs obtained from the various sources just enumerated have formed the basis of the reproductions which will be found in the volume.

The process by which they have been engraved was selected as being distinctly the best in existence for relief printing, and a more satisfactory result has, we think, been obtained than could be hoped for from the highest development of engraving on wood.

Our thanks are due in an especial degree to Mr. A. W. Franks, not only for the assistance tendered in connection with the collection in the British Museum, to which he has so largely and generously contributed, but also for the records, derived from private sources, which he has kindly furnished.

To M. Solon, Dr. Norris, Dr. Blackmore, Mr. A. Hartshorne, and other collectors and curators of museums who have courteously afforded useful information, but whom space forbids us to mention by name, we desire to tender our grateful acknowledgments. For the technical details connected with the production of the volume, notably those of the paper, printing, and process of reproduction, we are under great obligations to our friend Mr. Bale (of Messrs. Cassell and Company, Limited), whose cordial and appreciative co-operation in these matters has greatly contributed to what we venture to hope is from this technical point of view a successful result.

We deeply regret that the tardy appearance of our volume has prevented the recognition in their lifetime of the help, most valuable in some cases, rendered by the following collectors, who have during its progress joined the majority:—Mr. Toplis, of Nottingham; Mr. Soden Smith, of the South Kensington Museum; Mr. Fisher, of Midhurst; Mr. Smith, of Wisbech; and last but not least, Mr. W. Edkins, of Bristol, a well-known and indefatigable collector, to whom, although of advanced years, the possession of each new piece gave the keenest pleasure, and whose collection, recently dispersed, contained many covetable specimens. Mr. Edkins warmly sympathised with our undertaking, freely giving us the fullest possible information; and it will be seen that we drew largely on his stores. We greatly regret that he did not live to see the reproduction of his most favourite specimens.

In conclusion, we crave the indulgence of our subscribers in their estimate of our work.

Of its imperfections and shortcomings we fully expect to be reminded, and shall take in good part all friendly criticism. We only ask for a recognition of our good faith in endeavouring to give of our best to those who have responded to our invitation, and shall feel amply rewarded if we succeed in imparting a measure of information and enjoyment to the lovers of all illustrations, however homely, of the domestic history of our glorious past.

J. E. H.

Childwall, Richmond-on-Thames.
September, 1891.

EARLY ENGLISH POTTERY.

UNCERTAIN GLAZED.

1571. (No. 1.) A Puzzle Jug; red body, coated with green glaze, partially worn off. Dated in relief—

1571

Height 6½ *in.; diameter* 3½ *in.*

COLL. M.P.G.

1611.
1612. (No. 2.) A Tyg with four handles, each with three loops; red body, with brilliant dark brown glaze approaching black. Decoration impressed in outline. This and the two following pieces are of great interest, as they represent the nobler form of the ordinary tyg, which, for a long period, was the usual drinking-vessel of the country, and of which specimens are frequently turned up in a mutilated form during excavations. These four-handled tygs were doubtless loving-cups, out of which four persons drank on festive occasions. Inscribed below the rim with date and what appear to be initials, and below, above the base, with another date of a year later.

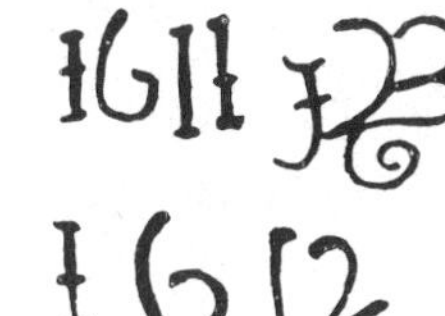

Height 7 *in.; diameter* 4¾ *in.*

B. MUS. (*WILLETT COLL.*).

1640. (No. 3.) A similar Tyg; with impressed ornament, including a crowned harp, rose, and thistle. Inscribed with initials and date—

ANO ES MAY. 1640

Height 5½ *in.; diameter* 4¾ *in.*
Coll. *B. Mus.*

1645. (No. 4.) A similar Tyg; also with the crowned rose, harp, and thistle. This vessel has a hole leading down from one of the knobs on the handles and communicating with the bottom, but it is difficult to see how it could have been used as a Puzzle Jug. Inscribed with initials and date—

DECEMB: THE OFIRST:
1645
S
MM

Height 6 *in.; diameter* 5 *in.*
Coll. *J.E.H.*

1671. (No. 5.) A Large Jug, of brown glaze; inscribed in raised black letters with initials and date—

Height 13¼ *in.; diameter* 9 *in.*
Coll. *B. Mus.*

16 R 71
EE

1680. (No. 6.) A Large Jug, of dark brown glaze; inscribed with initials and date, incised—

Height 13 *in.; diameter* 11 *in.*
Coll. *J.S.*

1680 T I M

1691. (No. 7.) A Puzzle Jug; coarse brown body, coated with green lead glaze. Neck pierced; handle enclosing a channel leading from the bottom of the vessel to the rim, where it opens in three spouts. An incised inscription around the body—

John Hedg Wood 1691

Height 5 *in.*
Coll. *M.P.G.*

1716. (No. 8.) A very large Harvest Jug; dark brown glaze; inscribed with motto and date—

HERE Y.OV MAY SEE WHAT I REQVST OF HANST
GENTL MEN MY BALY FILED OF THE BAST
I COM BVT NOW AND THEN 1716

Height 14 *in.; diameter* 10 *in.* *B. Mus.* (*Willett Coll.*).

1718. (No. 9.) A Puzzle Jug, covered with dark brown glaze; inscribed near the upper margin with initials and date—

A M
17.1.8

Height 6 *in.;*
diameter $5\frac{1}{2}$ *in.*
Coll. T. Mus.

1720. (No. 10.) A Pot with lid; of blackish glaze; resembles Nos. 2, 3, and 4. One handle with six double loops and rosettes; inscribed with initials and date—

AA 1720

B. Mus.

1723. (No. 11.) A Jug, with spout in form of mask. Brilliant glaze of extremely dark brown. Inscription raised in a dotted pattern. Said to have been made in Wales.

Fine Ale
i C C
1723

Height $9\frac{3}{4}$ *in.;*
diameter 7 *in.*
Coll. J.E.H.

(No. 12.) A Flask (*temp.* Henry VIII.); imperfect; green glaze, decorated with ornaments in relief. On one side, Royal Arms within garter, on a rose. Inscription near edge. Has been a costrel with long neck and four loops. Found in London. DN̄E · SALVVM · FAC · REGEM REGINAM · ET · REGNUM. On the other side monogram, the word LEAL, and rosettes.

Present height 8 *in.* Coll. B. Mus.

(No. 13.) A Puzzle Tyg, with three handles; purplish glaze; decorated with a mermaid, and inscribed with initials—

FV

Height 7 *in.; diameter* 7 *in.*

B. Mus. (*Franks Coll.*).

(No. 14.) A Puzzle Tyg, with three handles; dark green glaze; ornamented in relief. Inscribed on one side with merchant's mark—

Height 6½ *in.; diameter* 4¾ *in.*

B. Mus. (*Franks Coll.*).

(No. 15.) A brown globular Jug or Bottle; incised inscription—

Bells of Ouseley.

Height 9 *in.; diameter* 7 *in.*

B. Mus. (*Willett Coll.*).

SLIP-DECORATED WARE.

THIS ware owes its origin mainly to *Staffordshire*, which has undoubtedly furnished the largest number of extant specimens, to *Kent*, in which county one pottery (that of Wrotham) has given us some of our choicest pieces, and lastly, to *Cheshire* and *Derbyshire*, where this kind of pottery was produced up to a comparatively late period. The earliest dated specimen we have met with was made in 1612, at Wrotham; the latest dated Wrotham being 1710. The material of the body of this ware was usually a coarse reddish clay, on which, when formed by the wheel or otherwise, *slip*, a thin creamy mixture of clay and water, was allowed to trickle through a small tube by the workman, who thus produced, according to his fancy, quaint figures, conventional designs, borders, medallions, inscriptions, names, or dates. A glaze, usually composed of sulphuret of lead, often mixed with manganese, was then applied before firing, and this gave to the body and to the slip, of whatever colour, the rich yellow tone and transparency which adds so much to the charm of the ware. The vessels decorated with slip comprise tygs, posset-pots, cups, jugs, plates, dishes, candlesticks, and cradles intended for gifts. Although the specimens made at Wrotham are not the most numerous, they are, as a rule, the most elaborately decorated, medallions and rosettes being of frequent occurrence. It has been stated that one Jull was an eminent potter at Wrotham, where the name still survives, and the letters "H.I." on four pieces recorded in our list, and "T.I." on two other specimens, may perhaps stand for the initials of the potters' names. The letters "I.E." are *very* frequently (and "G.R." occasionally) met with; and if, as M. Solon asserts, John Evelyn, cousin of the diarist, owned the site of the manufactory, the picturesque remains of which are still to be seen, it is possible that these initials bore reference to him. All our enquiries made on the spot in the hope of tracing a connection between the Evelyns and the "I.E." have, however, proved unsuccessful. The Staffordshire potters, Thomas and Ralph Toft, have left us many reminders of their existence, in the shape, principally, of large dishes, fully illustrated in this volume. Only one dated piece of the former seems to be known, No. 43, inscribed "166—," the last figure having been obliterated. Ralph Tofts run from 1676 to 1683, and many undated specimens of his quaint, uncouth, yet picturesque work survive. His name is intimately connected with the Staffordshire pottery district, and one at least of the family is still potting. The fashion of signing the large plates for which the Tofts were famous was followed, as will be seen, by many of their fellows. The pieces made at Cockpit Hill, notices of several of which will be found in these pages, are mainly due to the Myers, or Miers (1708 and later dates). The Heaths were also connected with this pottery centre. To a large extent produced by a combination of moulded outlines and slip fillings, the decoration of this ware is exceptionally picturesque and attractive, but for this very reason has somewhat less of wildness and extravagance than those types in which the workman, uneducated and illiterate as a rule, had a perfectly free hand. Of a less decorative character than most of the slip-decorated pieces is the ware which we have classed, in accordance with Mr. Franks' views, as *Metropolitan Slip*, the pieces in this group having been mainly found in or near London. The glaze is less brilliant and the inscriptions are less boldly raised than in the Kentish or Staffordshire Slip pieces, and we have only come across four dated specimens, of the years 1650, 1651, 1659, and 1730.

1612. Wrotham. (No. 16) A Tyg with four double handles; rich warm brown glaze, decorated in yellow slip. Inscribed with initials and date in cartouches. A very fine and early specimen—

Height 7½ *in.; width* 4⅞ *in.*
COLL. L. MUS.

1621. Wrotham. (No. 17.) A large Four-handled Tyg. Body chocolate-coloured, ornamented with rude medallions in pale yellow, embossed with a rose, fleur-de-lys, lion rampant, and quatrefoils. Inscribed with initials and date—

Height 6½ *in.; diameter of rim* 4 *in.*
COLL. M.P.G.

1627. **Wrotham.** (No. 18.) A Tyg with four double handles of decorative character; brown glaze, ornamented with medallions enclosing date, initials, rose, and fleur-de-lys—

1627 | I L

Height 6 *in.; diameter* $4\frac{1}{2}$ *in.*
B. MUS. (FRANKS COLL.).

1630. **Wrotham.** (No. 19.) A Mug; rich brown glaze, decorated in yellow slip. Inscribed with legend and date—

FEARE GOD

1630

Height 5 *in.; diameter* $3\frac{3}{4}$ *in.*
COLL. G. ST.

1638. **Wrotham.** (No. 20.) A small Tyg with four double handles; dark-brown glaze, decorated very slightly in yellow slip. Inscribed with initials and date. A very picturesque and pretty piece.

IL MN 1638

Height 5 *in.; diameter* 4 *in.*
B. MUS. (WILLETT COLL.).

1642. (No. 21.) "A Quart Drink Mug," with four handles, double looped; between the handles are ornaments in pale slip. Inscribed with initials and date. Mentioned by Mr. Shaw.

GR 1642 MH

In 1824 this piece was in the possession of Mr. Richard Keys, and had been in his family for a century.

1643. **Cock Pit Hill.** (No. 22.) A Dish of very unusual character; brown glaze, "pie-crust" edge, ornamented with fleur-de-lys between four fishes. Inscribed with initials and date—

DA 1643

Diameter $13\frac{1}{4}$ *in.*
B. Mus. (*Willett Coll.*).

1649. (No. 23.) A Candlestick; rich brown glaze, ornamented with pattern of dots in white slip. Inscribed with initials and date—

1649:EM:T

Height 7 *in.; diameter of base* $5\frac{1}{2}$ *in.*
Coll. M.P.G.

1650. **Wrotham.** (No. 24.) A Tyg with four handles; dark brown glaze decorated in yellow slip. Inscribed with initials and date—

GR 1650

Height $5\frac{3}{4}$ *in.; diameter* $5\frac{1}{4}$ *in.* *B. Mus.* (*Franks Coll.*).

1650. **Metropolitan Slip.** (No. 25.) A Jar of elegant shape, recently dug up in the excavations near Bishopsgate Street for the Great Eastern Railway Company's extension—

* THE GIFT IS SMALL
GOOD WILL IS ALL 1650

Height 6 *in.; diameter* 4 *in.* COLL. G. MUS.

1650. (No. 26.) A Circular Dish, inscribed with maker's name and date in rude letters of a different clay. Mentioned by Mr. Shaw.

THOMAS SANS
1650

1651. **Metropolitan Slip.** (No. 27.) A Pot with Handle; brown glaze, inscribed in yellow slip with legend and date—

BREAK ME NOT I PRAY IN
YOVER HAST FOR I TO NON
WILL GIVE DES TAST 1651

Height $6\frac{7}{8}$ *in.; diameter* $7\frac{5}{8}$ *in.* COLL. L. MUS.

1651. (No. 28.) A Candlestick, with double set of four loops or handles; brown glaze, decorated with dots of yellow slip. Inscribed round the top, middle, and base with initials and date. (*See* No. 23 for similar specimen in M.P.G.)

1651 GR SAS

Height 11 *in.*
B. Mus. (*Willett Coll.*).

1651. **Wrotham.** (No. 29.) A Candlestick; companion to No. 28, in British Museum. Inscribed with initials and date—

1651 BE MH GR

Height 10 *in.* COLL. *H.G.*

1651. **Wrotham.** (No. 30.) A Jug, with one handle; brown glaze, decorated with yellow slip. Inscribed with initials and date—

Height 10 *in.; diameter* 6 *in.*
COLL. LORD DE L.

1653. **Wrotham.** (No. 31.) A Puzzle Tyg, with three handles; brown glaze, decorated in yellow. Inscribed with initials and date—

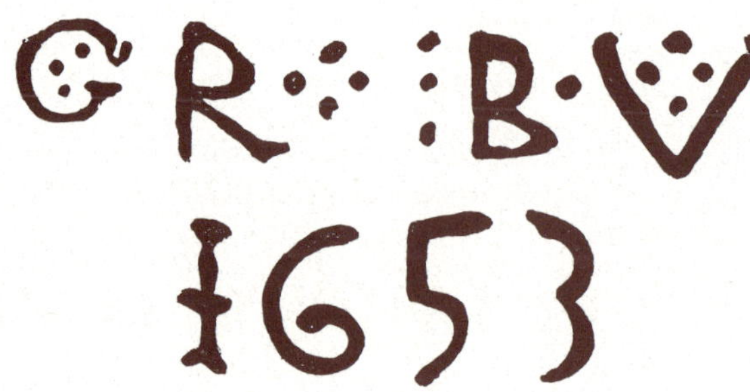

Height 3¼ *in.; diameter* 3 *in.* B. *MUS.* (*WILLETT COLL.*)

1654. **Wrotham.** (No. 32.) A Posset-Pot, with four double handles; brown glaze, decorated in yellow with fleur-de-lys and other ornament, and inscribed with initials and date. The initials are supposed to be those of the Wrotham potter Thomas Jull, and the piece is still in the possession of a member of the family.

T.I. 1654

Height 6½ *in.; diameter* 5½ *in.*
COLL. *W.J.*

1656. **Wrotham.** (No. 33.) A Jug of globular form, with one handle; brown glaze, decorated in yellow slip with ornaments and panels containing initials and date.

Height 5¼ *in.; diameter* 5¼ *in.* COLL. *M. MUS.*

1656. **Wrotham.** (No. 34.) A Posset-Pot, with four double handles; brown glaze, decorated with yellow, and inscribed with initials and date. This Pot is supposed to have been made for one Nicholas Haddock, and the initials to stand for his name.

N.H. 1656

Height 6½ *in.; diameter* 5½ *in.*
Coll. E.J.

1656. (No. 35.) A Bowl; buff-coloured glaze, with brown and green ornaments, in relief, of a heart, hour-glass, skull, etc.; rising from the centre are two clasped hands, and four handles project from the rim; incised inscription and date. This piece has been ascribed by high authorities to an English source, but the design, colouring, and even inscriptions strongly incline us to attribute to it a foreign origin.

Diameter 8 *in.* *Coll. S.K.M.*

PP C·
ANNO
1656

1656. **Wrotham.** (No. 36.) A Candlestick, with six nozzles, one of which is broken, as is also the base; greenish-brown glaze, decorated with yellow slip dots. Inscribed with initials and date in same colour. Similar to No. 23.

IW : I656 :

B. Mus. (*Willett Coll.*).

1657. **Wrotham.** (No. 37.) A Jug of globular form, with one handle; brown glaze, decorated in yellow slip with ornaments and panels containing initials and date. Similar to No. 33.

Height 5¾ *in.;*
diameter 3½ *in.*

HI 1657

Coll. M. Mus.

1659. **Wrotham.** (No. 38.) A fine Tyg, with four double handles and whistle; rich brown glaze, decorated with yellow slip. Inscribed with legend and date—

WROTHAM 1659 GR

RWS

Height 6½ *in.; diameter* 5 *in.* *Coll. Lord de L.*

An exactly similar specimen was in the possession of the late Mr. Baldwin.

1659. **Metropolitan Slip.** (No. 39.) A Cup, with one handle; brown glaze; inscribed in yellow slip with legend and date—

FAST
AND PRAY
1659

Height 4¾ *in.; diameter* 2½ *in.*
B. Mus. (*Franks Coll.*).

1659. **Wrotham.** (No. 40.) A Puzzle Tyg, with four handles and spout; brown glaze, decorated with yellow slip. Inscribed with initials and date—

I W 1659

Height 5¼ *in.; diameter* 4¾ *in.*
B. Mus. (*Willett Coll.*).

1659. (No. 41.) A Tyg; inscribed with date; mentioned by Mr. Marryatt.

1659. **Wrotham.** (No. 42.) A fine Tyg, with four triple handles; brown glaze, decorated with yellow slip in the usual Wrotham style. Inscribed with initials and date—

EST B NH
E M 1663

Height 7¼ *in.; diameter* 5¾ *in.*
B. Mus. (*Willett Coll.*).

166–. (No. 43.) A Dish; inscribed on the front, in slip, with the maker's name, on the back inscription and date scratched in—

THOMASTOFT

Tinker's Clough. I made it. 166–

Mentioned by M. Solon as having been seen in a cottage at Hanley.

1664. **Cock Pit Hill.** (No. 44.) A large Dish of variegated colour; decorated with a sun surrounded by fleur-de-lys and a conventional border. Name and date incised on the back—

JOSEPH KING
CW 1664

Diameter 15½ *in.*

COLL. B. MUS.

1668. **Wrotham.** (No. 45.) A large Brown Dish, decorated with incised pattern, and inscribed with initials and date. Mentioned by Mr. Jewitt.

HL IA 1668

1668. (No. 46.) An Owl Cup, without lid which formed the head; rich yellow glaze, decorated with dots in lighter slip. Inscribed on the breast with initials and date, incised, enclosed in a heart-shaped medallion.

HI F
668

Height 10½ *in.*

B. MUS. (WILLETT COLL.).

1669. **Wrotham.** (No. 47.) A Puzzle Jug of quaint shape, with figure of a man seated on the spout; brown glaze, decorated in yellow slip, and inscribed with initials and date—

Height $6\frac{1}{2}$ *in.*
Coll. *B. Mus.*

1671. **Cock Pit Hill.** (No. 48.) A Porringer with two handles; decorated with figure of a cock, and inscribed with date—

Diameter $6\frac{1}{4}$ *in.*
Coll. *F.M.H.*

1675. **Wrotham.** (No. 49.) A Two-handled Posset-Pot; rich brown glaze, decorated in yellow slip; on one side a crown, on the other the initials C.R., also three impressions from a seal of armorial bearings.

Height 5 *in.; diameter* $4\frac{3}{4}$ *in.*
Coll. *A.E.C.*

1675. (No. 50.) A Tablet; light brown glaze, inscribed in yellow slip with initials and date. Mentioned by Miss Meteyard.

1676. (No. 51.) A large Dish; yellow glaze, decorated in dull red slip with figure of a large bird. Inscribed in dark brown with maker's name and date—

RALPH TOFT 1676

Diameter 18 *in.* *B. Mus.* (*Willett Coll.*).

1676. (No. 52.) A Dish; decorated in the centre with the figures of a lady and gentleman, and inscribed on the border with maker's name and date as above.

Coll. Salford Mus.

1677. (No. 53.) A large Dish; yellow glaze, decorated in dull red slip with the figure of a man with sword. Inscribed in dark brown as above, with maker's name and date.

Diameter 17 *in.* *B. Mus.* (*Willett Coll.*).

1678. (No. 54.) A Three-handled Posset-Pot of brown glaze, elaborately decorated in a darker brown relieved with yellow and impressed with various patterns. The upper portion is also decorated with a ram's-horn ornament, the lower part panelled vertically. The cup was evidently made by R. M. for Mary Humphreys, and the local pronunciation is doubtless indicated by the phonetic spelling.

Height 8½ *in.; diameter* 7¾ *in.*

Coll. J.E.H.

MARY ||
OVMFARIS ||
YOVRICVP || 1678 | RM |

1678. **Wrotham.** (No. 55.) A "Fountain"; dark olive-brown glaze, decorated and inscribed in yellow slip; the royal arms embossed on a medallion in the centre. Inscribed with legend and date.

W
W : : E
THE:RIT:CENNRAL:JORNAL:
OFER:THE:DROVNK:KEN:
REGMENT:NH:1678:

Height 13½ *in.; diameter* 10½ *in.* B. MUS. (WILLETT COLL.).

1680. (No. 56.) A Cup; yellow glaze, decorated in brown slip dotted with yellow. Inscribed with name and date.

RICHARD : 1680 :

Height 3⅞ *in.; diameter* 3⅞ *in.* COLL. L. MUS.

168–. (No. 57.) A Two-handled Cup; the lower half in combed ware, the upper yellow glaze. Inscribed and dated in brown letters dotted with yellow slip.

RALPH : TVRNOR
168

Height 5 *in.; diameter* 6 *in.*
B. MUS. (WILLETT COLL.).

1682. (No. 58.) A Two-handled Posset-Pot; body pale yellow, marbled brown, with stamped ornaments. Inscribed in compartments round the neck with initials and date—

RF IG · MC RD 1682

Height 5½ *in.; diameter* 5 *in.* COLL. *M.P.G.*

1682. (No. 59.) A Six-handled Posset-Pot; dark brown glaze, decorated in yellow slip, and inscribed in dotted letters with legend and date—

ANN : BRIT :
HER : CVP ·
1682

Height 5½ *in.; diameter* 6½ *in.* COLL. *N. MUS.*

1683. (No. 60.) A Two-handled Posset-Pot with cover; light brown glaze, streaked with a darker shade. Inscribed with maker's name and date—

RALPH TOFT 1683

Height 6¼ *in.; diameter* 6¼ *in.* COLL. *BED. M.*

1684. (No. 61.) A Four-handled Tyg; dark brown glaze, decorated on the lower part with vertical, serrated, and twisted strips in yellow slip. Inscribed with name and date—

MARGRETE COLLEY
1684

Height 6¾ *in.* COLL. *L.M.S.*

1685. (No. 62.) A large Circular Dish of very unusual character; dark slip decoration on yellow glaze, central female figure with quaint coiffure, long wasp-like body, and bell-shaped skirts, holding her hands over two smaller figures similarly attired. Serpentine border on edge—

1685

Diameter 18½ *in.*
COLL. T. MUS.

1687. **Wrotham.** (No. 63.) A Double-handled Posset-Pot; body dark brown, ornamented in yellow slip with fleur-de-lys. Inscribed with initials and date—

IE 1687 EC

Height 6 *in.*; *diameter* 6½ *in.* COLL. M.P.G.

1688. (No. 64.) A Two-handled Posset-Pot; yellow glaze, decorated with conventional flowers in brown slip, with yellow dots. Inscribed round rim with initials and date—

EP || RF || WS ||
TD || AI || TG || 1688 ||

Height 5 *in.*; *diameter* 6½ *in.*
B. MUS. (WILLETT COLL.).

1688. (No. 65.) A large Dish; yellow glaze, decorated in brown slip, with raised figures of birds, etc., in centre, and two heads—of a gentleman and lady. Inscribed along rim, under portraits, with legend and date—

RICHARD:PERIN:
DARITY:PERIN
1688

Diameter 18 *in.*

Coll. F.P.

1690. (No. 66.) A Puzzle Tyg, with six handles; bright red glaze, decorated in yellow slip, the light clay in places being coloured with copper-green. Ornamented with stars and rosettes and innumerable knobs.

IOHN:HVGH:1690

Coll. L.M.S.

1691. (No. 67.) A Dish; yellow glaze, with brick-red and dark-brown decoration; all the lines a dark brown, the inside of the leaves and berries with which it is ornamented being brick-red, and dotted with white round the edges. Inscribed with initials, legend, and date—

W S

THIS:FoR:W:F: 1691

Diameter $17\frac{1}{2}$ *in.* *Coll. F.B.*

1692. (No. 68.) A fine Tyg, with three handles and the remains of a spout up one side. The lower half dark brown glaze, decorated with conventional ornaments in yellow slip; the upper half yellow glaze, inscribed with legend and date in brown slip dotted with yellow.

Height $6\frac{1}{2}$ *in.; diameter* $7\frac{1}{2}$ *in.*
B. *Mus.* (Franks Coll.).

ROBART SHAW : 1692

1692. (No. 69.) A Tablet; ornament and decoration on margin in yellow slip. Inscribed with initials and date, the initials being those of Burslem Wedgwood, and the tablet built into the wall of a house formerly belonging to him—once a farmhouse, now a joiner's shop.

B ◦ W ◦ 1692 ◦

1692. (No. 70.) A Dutch Oven; brown glaze; decoration and date in yellow slip.

1692

Length 9 *in.*
Coll. B. *Mus.*

1693. (No. 71.) A Jug, with a figure of Plenty modelled in front. Inscribed round the rim with initials and date. The inscription is very indistinct.

I.B. I.O.N.N.1693 Coll. H. *Mus.*

1693. (No. 72.) A small Cradle, elaborately ornamented; rich reddish-brown glaze, decorated in buff and black. Inscribed with date on the top. Mentioned by Mr. Jewitt.

1693

Height $4\frac{3}{4}$ *in.*; *length* $7\frac{3}{4}$ *in.*

1694. (No. 73.) A large Dish; yellow glaze, decorated with grotesque portraits in brown slip; border of the usual trellis pattern. Inscribed with name and date—

JAMES JOHNSON 1694

The date may perhaps be 1691. *Diameter* 17 *in.* COLL. *N.C. Mus.*

1694. (No. 74.) A Jug; rich brown glaze, decorated with a flower in yellow slip, and inscribed with date—

1694

Height 4 *in.*; *diameter* $3\frac{3}{4}$ *in.* COLL. *J.F.*

1695. (No. 75.) A large Two-handled Posset-Pot; yellow glaze, decorated in brown dotted with yellow slip. Flowers in panels. Inscribed with legend and date—

THE·BEST·IS·NOT·TO·
GOOD·FOR·YOV·1695·

Height $5\frac{1}{2}$ *in.*; *diameter* 14 *in.* COLL. *F.P.*

1695. **Uncertain Slip.** (No. 76.) An odd-looking piece, of triangular form, which is probably a stand for a flat-iron; though a very good authority considers it may be a head-stone for a tomb.

1695
E • E
When • this • V • C
Remember . mee

Length $7\frac{3}{4}$ *in.*
B. Mus. (*Meyrick Coll.*).

1696. (No. 77.) A large Two-handled Posset-Pot; the lower half dark brown glaze decorated in yellow slip with crude conventional design; a band of dark brown glaze dotted with yellow slip encircling the top; whilst the middle consists of a very rich yellow glaze, inscribed with name and date in brown dotted letters. A very fine specimen.

WILLIAM : CHATERLY : 1696 :

Height 7 *in.; diameter* $8\frac{3}{4}$ *in.* *B. Mus.* (*Willett Coll.*).

1697. **Wrotham.** (No. 78.) A Tyg with four double handles; rich brown glaze, decorated in yellow slip in the usual Wrotham style, with raised ornaments bordered with dots of yellow slip. Inscribed with initials and date—

IE
1697

Length $6\frac{1}{2}$ *in.; diameter* $6\frac{1}{4}$ *in.*
B. Mus. (*Willett Coll.*).

1697. (No. 79.) A Puzzle Jug; top and spout broken. Inscribed with date—

1697

Coll. H.G.

1697. (No. 80.) A Two-handled Posset-Pot; yellow glaze, decorated in brown slip with yellow dots. Inscribed with legend, initials, and date—

THE · BEST · IS · NOT · TOO ·
GOOD · FOR · YOV ⁞ 1697 ⁞ I · B · R · F ·

Height 5 *in.; diameter* 8 *in.* COLL. *G.S.*
A similar specimen. *Height* 7 *in.; diameter* 8 *in.*

1697. (No. 81.) A small Jug, of brown glaze with yellow slip decoration. Inscribed with initials and date—

IE : 1697

Height 3 *in; diameter* $3\frac{1}{3}$ *in.*
COLL. COL. *F.*

1697. (No. 82.) A Posset-Pot, with very rich floriated pattern. Inscribed with legend and date as above (*see* No. 80), but with different initials—

E · D · W · D · R · D · COLL. *H.G.*

1697. (No. 83.) A Two-handled Posset-Pot; yellow glaze, decorated in brown slip dotted with yellow. Inscribed with legend and date as above (*see* Nos. 80 and 82), but with different initials—

I · I I · B *Height* $5\frac{1}{2}$ *in.; diameter* $8\frac{1}{2}$ *in.*

1697. (No. 84.) A Puzzle Tyg, with top and spout broken. Inscribed with date—

1697

Coll. H.G.

1699. **Wrotham.** (No. 85) A beautiful Plate, of brown glaze, decorated with yellow slip. A curious mixture of slip and sgrafiato decoration. Inscribed with name, initials, and date—

IE : WE : 1699 :
WROT : HAM :

Diameter 21½ *in.*
Coll. B. Mus.

1699. (No. 86.) A small Cup with two handles; brown glaze, decorated in yellow slip dots, and inscribed with initials and date—

IE
: 1699

Height 3½ *in.; Diameter* 3½ *in.*
B. Mus. (*Willett Coll.*).

1700. (No. 87.) A Cup; the upper half in yellow glaze, decorated with initials and date in dark brown slip dotted with yellow; the lower half in combed ware. A very beautiful little piece.

I B

1700

Height $3\frac{1}{2}$ *in.; diameter* 3 *in.* COLL. *H.W.*

1700. (No. 88.) A large Cradle; yellow glaze, decorated in brown slip dotted with yellow; an inscription on each side, and a crowned effigy surmounting the date at the end.

WILLIAM : SMITH
MARTHA : SMITH
1700

Length 22 *in.* COLL. *L.M.S.*

1702. (No. 89.) A Dish, mentioned by M. Solon. Inscribed with maker's name and date—

W · RICH · 1702

Diameter 20 *in.*

1702. (No. 90.) A Two-handled Posset-Pot; buff-coloured glaze, slightly decorated in dark brown slip, and inscribed in same with name and date in letters alternately dotted—

IOB : HEATH : 1702

Height $4\frac{3}{4}$ *in.; diameter* $6\frac{3}{4}$ *in.* COLL. PROF. *W.*

1703. Wrotham. (No. 91.) A Double-handled Posset-Pot, in coarse red earthenware, with ornaments; inscription and date in yellow slip.

I·E·1703
WROTHAM

Height 4¾ *in.; diameter* 4¼ *in.*
COLL. *M.P.G.*

1703. Wrotham. (No. 92.) A Double-handled Posset-Pot; an almost exactly similar specimen to the above—mentioned and illustrated by M. Solon. Inscribed with the same name, initials, and date.

1703. (No. 93.) A Cradle; inscribed with maker's name and date—

JOSEPH GLASS 1703

Length 10 *in.* COLL. *H.G.*

1704. (No. 94.) A large Dish; yellow glaze, decorated in reddish slip with good conventional design and the usual trellis border. Inscribed with name and date. A very fine plate, the ornament of a higher quality than is usual in this ware.

MARY:PERKINS:
1704:

Diameter 8½ *in.* B. MUS. (WILLETT COLL.).

1704. Wrotham. (No. 95.) A Cylindrical Vase and Cover; brown glaze, decorated in the usual Wrotham style in yellow slip. Two knobs serve as handles. Inscribed with initials and date—

I E   1704

Height $9\frac{1}{2}$ *in.; diameter* 5 *in.*
B. Mus. (*Willett Coll.*).

1704. (No. 96.) A large Jug, no doubt a presentation piece; an imitation of Thomas Toft's ware, if not a work of his own hand. The clay and slip are the same as those of the Toft dishes, and the brown outline is dotted over with the customary white specks; on each side a bird, perhaps meant for a peacock, is perched upon a branch, and a monogram and date are inscribed on the neck—

AS 1704

Height $9\frac{1}{2}$ *in.; diameter* 5 *in.* *Coll. L.M.S.*

1705. (No. 97.) A Tyg, with four handles; yellow glaze, decorated in brown slip dotted with yellow. Inscribed with name and date—

MARY : SHIFILBOTTOM : 1705

Height $9\frac{1}{2}$ *in.* *Coll. L.M.S.*

1707. (No. 98.) A Three-handled Posset-Pot; black glaze, inscribed with name and date in yellow slip—

ELLYN:
WYLLCOCKSON:1707:

Height 7 *in.; diameter* 8 *in.*

1707. (No. 99.) A Tyg, with three handles; the upper part covered with yellow glaze, having inscription in brown slip; the lower part covered with brown glaze, decorated in yellow slip. Inscribed with legend and date. A very similar piece to No. 179.

ANN:DRAPER:THIS:
CVP:I:MADE FOR:YOV:
AND:SO:NO:MORE:I:W:
1707::

Height 6½ *in.; diameter* 9 *in.*
B. Mus. (*Willett Coll.*).

1707. **Wrotham.** (No. 100.) A small Puzzle Tyg, with three handles; rich reddish-brown glaze, decorated in yellow slip. Inscribed with initials and date—

:I E:1707

Height 3½ *in.; diameter* 3½ *in.* *B. Mus.* (*Franks Coll.*).

1707. Wrotham. (No. 101.) A Two-handled Tyg; brown glaze, decorated in yellow slip, and inscribed with name, initials, and date—

I:E:1707:
WROTHAM

Height $6\frac{1}{8}$ *in.; diameter* $6\frac{1}{4}$ *in.*
Coll. M. Mus.

1707. Wrotham. (No. 102.) A Two-handled Tyg; dated, with initials on medallion between handles; numerous emblems in relief.

(IE) 1707 W W S

Height $7\frac{1}{2}$ *in.; diameter* $7\frac{1}{4}$ *in.* *Coll. H.W.*

1707. (No. 103.) A Dish; yellow glaze, decorated in two shades of brown with figure of Queen Anne and conventional flowers; the rim ornamented with the usual trellis pattern, and inscribed with name and date.

IOHN · WRIGH · J707

The T evidently omitted by mistake.

Diameter $16\frac{3}{4}$ *in.* *Coll. W.L.B.*

1708. Cock Pit Hill. (No. 104.) A Three-handled Pot, holding about two gallons; coarse brown ware, glazed, inscribed with legend and date. Mentioned by Mr. Jewitt.

Drink be merry and mary
God Bles creae George & Qveen ann
John Mier made this cvp 1708

1708. **Cock Pit Hill.** (No. 105.) A large Three-handled Posset-Pot; brown glaze, decorated and inscribed with yellow slip—

GOD:BLESS:THE:QVEEN:AND:PRENCE:
GORGE.DRINK:AND:BE:MERRY:AND:MARRY:
BB:IOHN:MEIR:MADE:THIS:CVP:1708

B. Mus. (*Franks Coll.*).

1708. (No. 106.) A Three-handled Tyg; reddish-brown glaze, decorated in yellow slip. Inscribed with legend and date—

RICHARD:MEIR:
HIS:CVP:1708:

(*See* Note at end of volume for history of this piece.)

1709. (No. 107.) A Dish of the usual Toft character, with trellis or chequer pattern on rim; in highly glazed yellow and brown slip. In the centre a crowned female figure holding a flower in each hand. At either side of the head the initials q A (Queen Anne).

WILLIAM:WRIGHT:
1709

Diameter 16¼ *in.*
Coll. *J.E H*

1710. Wrotham. (No. 108.) A Bell-shaped Cup, with two handles similar to No. 101. The centre is decorated with raised figures, etc., and the remainder of the surface covered with ornaments and dots. The initials "T. B" occur in two places, also the letters "I E" between the handles.

IE 1710

T.B

Height 7 in. COLL. LATE *W.E.*

1710. Wrotham. (No. 109) A large Posset-Pot, with two knobs serving as handles; body dark brown glaze, ornamented in yellow slip with fleur-de-lys. Inscribed with initials and date—

I E 1710

Height 7 in.; diameter $5\frac{1}{2}$ *in.*

COLL. *M.P.G.*

1710. **Wrotham.** (No. 110.) A Two-handled Pot; dark brown glaze, decorated with peculiar ornaments in yellow slip. Inscribed with legend and date. An unusual and very desirable piece.

IE
BB 1710
M

WROTHAM

Height 7 in.; diameter $6\frac{3}{4}$ *in.* *B. Mus.* (*Willett Coll.*).

1711. (No. 111.) A Posset-Pot, mentioned by Mr. Jewitt; the lower half in brown glaze, slightly decorated in yellow slip; the upper half in yellow glaze, decorated and inscribed in brown slip dotted with yellow.

GOD : SAVE : THE : QVEEN : 1711 :

1712. (No. 112.) A Two-handled Posset-Pot, arranged as a Puzzle Jug, with spouts at right angles to the handles. Cover with knob at apex. Brown glaze, elaborately decorated with patterns in slip of two colours, a pale and a darker yellow. Patterns principally geometrical, but also introducing a quadruped similar to those found in the first period of Etruscan decoration. The lower portion only has been glazed inside. Inscribed with name and date—

ELESSABATH :
HODGEIS : 1712 :

Height 12 *in.; diameter* $9\frac{1}{2}$ *in.* *Coll. J.E.H.*

1713. (No. 113.) A small Jug; yellow glaze; the lower half in combed decoration, the upper half divided into two compartments by band of brown dotted slip, and inscribed with initials and date—

D S : 1713 :

Height 4½ *in.*
B. Mus. (*Willett Coll.*).

1714. (No. 114.) A Posset-Pot with lid, and a spout at each side; inscription round the top in the usual dark slip letters, studded over with yellow dots. Inscribed with legend, initials and date—

THE BEST IS NOT TOO GOOD FOR YOU.
1714 · I L H

Height 9½ *in.* *Coll. L.M.S.*

1714. (No. 115.) A Four-handled Pot, with a cover in the shape of a crown; in rich brown glaze, decorated with horizontal rows of yellow slip dots alternately with an impressed star-like pattern. Inscribed with legend and date—

MARY PARVISH
her Pot 1714

Height 10 *in.; diameter* 6½ *in.*
B. Mus. (*Willett Coll.*).

1717. (No. 116.) A Two-handled Posset-Pot; rich red glaze, decorated in light yellow slip with dots and rosettes. Inscribed with initials and date—

1717
MFE

IE

Height 10 *in.; diameter* 6½ *in.*
B. Mus. (*Willett Coll.*).

1719. (No. 117.) A small Jug; dark-brown glaze, decorated with very large yellow spots (not raised); a band of light yellow running round the rim. Inscribed with date in yellow slip—

1719

Height $3\frac{3}{4}$ *in.* *B. Mus.* (*Willett Coll.*).

1721. (No. 118.) A Bottle; dark red body, the greater portion covered with dark brown glaze, the very lowest part left unglazed. Inscribed with initials and date in yellow slip—

I : C

1721

Height 8 *in.*
Coll. L. Mus.

1725. (No. 119.) A Cradle; coated over with red clay rudely incised, and covered with manganese glaze—

The Gufl Is fmall But
loue ys all Calron whelecors
1725

Length 10 *in.* *Coll. L.M.S.*

1726. **Cock Pit Hill.** (No. 120.) A Dish, representing a plant with a single stem, from which spring branches and leaves on either side of the medallion in centre which contains the inscription; above the medallion is a hand grasping a large bird, on either side perches a smaller one.

SM
one
burd:in
The:hand
is Worth
Two:in:the
buch
17 26

Diameter $14\frac{1}{2}$ *in.* *B. Mus.* (*Willett Coll.*).

1726. (No. 121.) A deep Dish; rich yellow glazed surface, brown and black slip; rude ornamentation; a female and winged angels blowing trumpets, and a pillar of salt. Inscribed with legend and date—

Remember
Lot's Wife
Luke:1732
1726

Diameter 14 *in.*
COLL. L.M.S.

1727. (No. 122.) A Plate; white glaze; inscription and decoration in dull red relief.

JOSEPH ::: MOSSON ::
THE : BEST : IS : NOT :
TOO : GOOD : FOR : YOV · 1727 :

Diameter $17\frac{1}{2}$ *in.* COLL. J.F.

1729. (No. 123.) A large Dish; light yellow glaze, decorated in rich brown slip with female figure, with arms upraised, holding a flower in each hand.

IM : MM 1729

Diameter 18 *in.* COLL. B. MUS.

1730. Metropolitan Slip. (No. 124.) A Two-handled Mug; yellow slip on red-glazed body; rude decoration. Inscribed with date—

1730

Height $4\frac{7}{8}$ *in.*; *diameter* $4\frac{7}{8}$ *in.*
COLL. J.E.H.

1730. (No. 125.) A Dish of light-coloured clay, covered on the inside with a yellow slip; moulded outline of a man on horseback above three leaves; the design is filled in with dark brown slip; on one side of the figure is a medallion with name and date in relief. The dish is notched round the edge.

Diameter 14¾ *in.*

COLL. L. MUS.

St
George
1730.

1732. (No. 126.) A small fragment of a grand Dish, now unfortunately comminuted, of a very unusual character, the letters being raised in relief. Probably made in commemoration of a funeral ceremony.

mber
6·Wife
1732

COLL. J.E.H.

1734. **Cock Pit Hill.** (No. 127.) A Dish; black glaze, ornamented with conventional foliage in cream-coloured and brown slip. On the rim is an inscription and date, also in cream-coloured slip. Initials in relief in the centre.

God:save:
King:George:
1734:S:M:1734

Diameter 14 *in.*

COLL. LATE W.E.

1735. (No. 128.) A Two-handled Posset-Pot; yellow glaze, decorated in brown slip; brown on lower part of the pot; combing under the inscription.

Height 5½ *in.; diameter* 6¾ *in.*
COLL. *J.E.H.*

1736. Cock Pit Hill. (No. 129.) A Circular Dish; black glaze, decorated with a stag in cream-coloured slip, the body filled in with brown glaze; a fern-leaf and butterfly complete the subject. Inscribed with date.

Diameter 11½ *in.* COLL. LATE *W.E.*

1740. (No. 130.) A Slip Bowl, inscribed with date.
COLL. *H.G.*

1744. (No. 131.) A large Circular Dish; brown glaze, decorated in yellow slip in a very quaint fashion. Two figures under a tree may possibly stand for the two spies. Large birds on the branches.

Diameter 17 *in.*

COLL. *J.F.*

1748. (No. 132.) A large Dish; brown glaze, decorated in yellow slip. This piece has a quaintly decorated margin, greatly resembling that of No. 131. The centre is occupied by the Royal Arms.

J748

Diameter 18½ *in.* Coll. *J.F.*

1749. (No. 133.) A Jug; ornamented with small squares, white and brown alternating. On the shoulder is a white band with brown, and initials and date. Parallel to each line of the letters is a line of dots. Below the shoulder the small squares occur again, and end in two white lines running round the jug.

W A J749

Height 6 *in.*
Coll. *Y. Mus.*

1749. **Cock Pit Hill.** (No. 134.) A Dish; brown glaze, decorated in yellow slip with figure of a cock on a bough. Inscribed with initials and date

W W
1749

Diameter 10¾ *in.* Coll. *L. Mus.*

1755. (No. 135.) A Pot with two handles: rich brown glaze, decorated slightly in yellow slip. Resembles Metropolitan Slip.

1755

Height $7\frac{1}{4}$ *in.; diameter* $7\frac{1}{2}$ *in.*
B. Mus. (*Willett Coll.*).

1762. (No. 136.) A Nest of Six Cups, with entwined handles; rich yellow glaze, mottled with green and brown. Inscribed with date, legend, and initials, in brown. (*See* Note at end of volume.)

"*fill me full drink of me while you woul*"
S 1762 O

Coll. late W.E.

1766. **Metropolitan Slip.** (No. 137.) A small Bowl, nearly hemispherical; brown glaze, inscribed in yellow slip with date, which covers most of the interior.

1766

Height $1\frac{1}{4}$ *in.; diameter* 4 *in.*
Coll. J.E.H.

1769. (No. 138.) A Dish; yellow glaze. Decorated with the figure of a bird, traced in brown. Inscribed with date.

Diameter 14 *in.* *Coll. L.M.S.*

1771. **Cock Pit Hill.** (No. 139.) A Two-handled Posset-Pot; yellow glaze, ornamented with brown marbled band. Inscribed on the rim in brown slip ornamented with yellow dots—

IOSHVA: HEATH 1771

Height 5 *in.; diameter of mouth* $6\frac{1}{2}$ *in.* *Coll. M.P.G.*

1771. **Cock Pit Hill.** (No. 140.) A large Dish; yellow glaze, decorated in brown slip with figure of a large bird surrounded by smaller ones. Indented edge to rim. Inscribed with date—

1771

Diameter 17½ *in.*

COLL. F.P.

1775. (No. 141.) A large Dish; brown glaze, decorated in yellow slip with a figure of a horse. Inscribed with date—

1775 *Diameter* 16 *in.* COLL. L.M.S.

1775. (No. 142.) A Dutch Oven; brown glaze. Decorated with wavy lines and date in yellow slip—

1775 COLL. LATE W.E.

1776. (No. 143.) A Fruit Stand, with large base; brown glaze, decorated in yellow slip with representation of fiddle and bow. A curious piece; resembles Metropolitan Slip.

Height 8 *in.*; *diameter* 8½ *in.* 1776 COLL. L. MUS.

1780. **Cock Pit Hill.** (No. 144.) A Circular Dish; black glaze, decorated in yellow slip with figure of a large bird on the wing. Inscribed with date—

1780

Diameter 11½ *in.* COLL. GEN. P.R., LATE W.E.

1781. (No. 145.) A Square Bottle, with four lobes; brown glaze, very slightly decorated with yellow slip, and inscribed in same colour with date—

1781

Height 10 *in.* COLL. *B. Mus.*

1794. **Cock Pit Hill.** (No. 146.) A large, flat Plate; very dark brown glaze, decorated in yellow slip with figure of a cock. Inscribed with date—

17
94

Diameter $15\frac{1}{2}$ *in.*
B. Mus. (*Willett Coll.*).

1798. (No. 147.) A large Jug; brown glaze, decorated in rich yellow slip. Decorated with a lion rampant, crowned, and the Union Jack; also foliage, and large, very conventional, flowers, and a large bird. Inscribed, on a medallion, with legend, date, and the maker's name, all scratched through the slip into the ware.

Despise me not
Because I'm made of clay
But make me wellcome
When I come this way
My Belly fill with good strong
Punch or Beer. And I will
Make you merry all the Year.

The Gift of
Rd. Wheeler
1798.

(Probably made in Wales or the West of England.)

Height $10\frac{1}{2}$ *in.* COLL. LATE *W.E.*

(No. 148.) A large Plate; yellow glaze; trellised border; geometrical border on dip of plate. In centre rude portraits of Catharine of Braganza, with the curled locks so conspicuous in her early portraits, and of Charles II. in wig and lace collar. Inscribed with maker's name—

THOMAS·TOFT

Diameter $17\frac{3}{4}$ *in.*
Coll. J.E.H.

(No. 149.) A large Dish; buff-coloured glaze, decorated in dark and light brown slip. In the centre a crowned lion, rampant, surrounded by trellised border. Inscribed with maker's name—

THOMAS TOFT

Diameter $17\frac{1}{2}$ *in.*
Coll. M.P.G.

(No. 150.) A large Plate; yellow glaze, decorated in the centre, in brown slip, with figure of a mermaid, mirror in left hand and comb in right. Trellised border, inscribed, like the preceding dish, with maker's name. *Diameter* $17\frac{1}{4}$ *in.* *Coll. S. K. Mus.*

(No. 151.) A Dish, mentioned by M. Solon; ornamented with a double-headed eagle, and inscribed, as above, with maker's name.

(No. 152.) A Dish; ornamented with a pelican, and inscribed, as above, with maker's name. Mentioned by M. Solon.

(No. 153.) A large Dish; yellow glaze, decorated in brown and orange slip with a lion and unicorn rampant. The rim of the usual trellis pattern, inscribed with maker's name. The initials T. L. in dotted letters also occur at the bottom of the plate below the figures.

Diameter 17¼ *in.* *Coll. S. K. Mus.*

(No. 154.) A very fine Dish; yellow glaze, ornamented in brown slip with lion and unicorn. Fine border. Inscribed, as above, with maker's name. *Diameter* 17 *in.* *Coll. B. Mus.*

(No. 155.) A Dish; decorated with figure of a cavalier drinking a toast, and inscribed, as above, with maker's name. *Coll. L.M.S.*

(No. 156.) A very large Dish; ornamented with half-length figure of Chas. II., and initials C. R. Inscribed, as above, with maker's name.
Diameter 22 *in.* *Coll. Bateman Mus.*

(No. 157.) A Dish; yellow glaze, decorated in centre, in brown slip, with figure, booted and spurred, holding, with arms upraised, a rose in each hand. Inscribed with maker's name, and initials R. W. in dotted letters on each side of the head.

Diameter 13 *in.* *Coll. F.B.*

(No. 158.) A very fine Dish; yellow glaze, decorated in the centre, in brown slip, with full-length figure of a man holding a staff in his hand. Conventional flowers and fleur-de-lys in the background. Inscribed below the figure with maker's name, and inscription at the left of head. Mentioned by M. Solon.

the
DVKE of
YORKE

thomAs toft

(No. 159.) A Dish, bearing the arms of King Charles, and inscribed (like preceding pieces) with maker's name. Mentioned by Mr. Marryatt as being in the collection of Lady Stafford.

(No. 160.) A Dish, mentioned by M. Solon; ornamented with conventional flowers, and inscribed, as above, with maker's name.

(No. 161.) A Circular Dish; decorated in cream-coloured slip in centre with lion rampant. Trellis border in yellow and brown. Inscribed, as above, with maker's name; the first four letters, however, of the Christian name having been chipped off. *Coll. Dub. Mus.*

(No. 162.) A Six-handled Tyg; brown glaze, decorated in black and yellow slip with pomegranates and head of Charles II. (C.R.) alternately between the handles. Inscribed on rim with name of maker and (?) intended possessor. A very uncommon piece for this maker.

THOMAS TOFT
ELISABETH POOT

Coll. Y. Mus.

(No. 163.) A Circular Dish; yellow glaze, decorated with figure of a lady holding a flower in her left hand. Outlines in black with white dots, interspaces filled in with orange slip. Trellis border inscribed with maker's name.

Diameter 16¾ *in.*
Coll. Gen. P.R., late W.E.

(No. 164.) A large Dish; yellow glaze, decorated, in dark and light brown slip, with a female figure and two crowned heads in ovals, with foliage, etc. A fine border, inscribed with maker's name—

RALPHOFT

Diameter 19 *in.*
Coll. L.M.S.

(No. 165.) A Two-handled Posset-Pot; the upper part of yellow glaze, decorated and inscribed with brown slip dotted with yellow; the lower part brown glaze, decorated with yellow slip. Inscribed with initials and maker's name—

IOSEPH GLASS : S : V : H G :

Height 6¾ *in.; diameter* 9¼ *in.* *B. Mus.* (*Franks Coll.*).

(No. 166.) A small Cradle, decorated with slip, and inscribed, as above, with maker's name, but without initials. *Coll. H.G.*

(No. 167.) A Cradle; brown glaze, decorated in yellow slip, and inscribed in same colour with maker's name—

RALPH · SIMPSON ·

Coll. L.M.S.

(No. 168.) A Dish, decorated with figures of William and Mary, and inscribed, as above, with maker's name. *Coll. L.M.S.*

(No. 169.) A Dish; coarse red ware, decorated with the device of a pelican in her piety, and a border of marks and medallions in brown slip on a yellow ground. Inscribed with maker's name—

RALPH·SIMPSON

Diameter 17 *in.* *Coll. S. K. Mus.*

(No. 170.) A Dish; yellow glaze, decorated in brown slip with an extremely crude and quaint attempt at a portrait. Inscribed, on the border, with the maker's name, and with the letters W. R. in dotted slip at either side of the bust.

Diameter 16 *in.*
B. Mus. (*Willett Coll.*).

(No. 171.) A remarkably fine Dish, decorated with two full-length figures in the costume of the Stuarts; the gentleman holding in his hand his hat and feather, and having "petticoat breeches," tied stockings, and high-heeled boots with ties, and the lady holding a bunch of flowers Initials W. T. between the figures and the rim. Inscribed at the bottom with the maker's name—

WILLIAM·TALOR

Diameter $17\frac{3}{4}$ *in.* — *B. Mus.* (*Willett Coll.*).

(No. 172). A large Dish, with two full-length portraits of William III. and Mary; yellow glaze, decorated in brown and orange slip. Inscribed on rim with maker's name—

WILLIAM TALOR

Diameter $17\frac{1}{8}$ *in.* — *Coll. L. Mus.*

(No. 173.) A large Dish; brown glaze, decorated in yellow slip. "It would be difficult," says M. Solon, "to be less realistic than George Taylor (who signed this dish) has been in his treatment of his royal group. He has evidently endeavoured to emulate Thomas Toft; the decoration is, however, still more primitive—in fact, anything more hideous than the two figures intended to represent the King and Queen it would be difficult to find."

GEORGE:TAYLOR

Diameter $16\frac{3}{4}$ *in.* — *Coll. L.M.S.*

(No. 174.) A very large Dish; yellow glaze, decorated in reddish-brown slip with stiff conventional design outlined with dots. Trellis border inscribed with maker's name.

IOHN·WRIGHT

Diameter 16 *in.* — *Coll. B. Mus.*

(No. 175.) **Cock Pit Hill.** A Three-handled Cup; yellow glaze, with rich decoration in brown slip dotted with yellow; the lower portion brown glaze, with pattern in yellow slip. Inscribed with maker's name. A beautiful and perfect specimen—

RICHARD
MEIR

Height $7\frac{3}{8}$ *in.; diameter* $9\frac{1}{4}$ *in.*
Coll. L. Mus.

(No. 176.) **Wrotham.** A very large Posset-Pot, with four double handles; reddish-brown glaze, decorated all over in orange slip with the usual Wrotham ornaments of rosettes and medallions, on one of which latter occur the arms of Amsterdam. The rim, which was once inscribed with legend, has been very much broken, so that only a few letters of inscription now remain—

WROT:HAM: N M

Height 9 *in.; diameter* 10 *in.* *B. Mus.* (*Willett Coll.*).

(No. 177.) **Wrotham.** A Two-handled Posset-Pot; brown glaze, decorated in the usual Wrotham style in yellow slip. Inscribed with initials and name—

IE
WROTHAM

Height 6 *in.; diameter* $6\frac{1}{4}$ *in.*
Coll. M. Mus.

(No. 178.) A Candlestick; red glaze, decorated and inscribed in yellow slip exactly like No. 23, in the Jermyn Street Museum. Inscribed with initials only—

HI MNT

Height $9\frac{1}{2}$ *in*; *diameter* $5\frac{1}{2}$ *in.* COLL. *M. MUS.*

(No. 179.) A large Three-handled Pot, with vertical raised bands between each handle; the upper portion covered with brilliant yellow glaze, and inscription in brown slip dotted with yellow; the lower part covered with brown glaze decorated in a rough conventional design with yellow slip. A very fine piece, evidently by the same maker as No. 99.

GEORGE:WARD:
MADE:THIS:CVP:AN:
D:SO:NO:MORE:BVT:GOD:BLESS:THE:
QVEEN:AND:ALL:HER:PARLEME:

Height 7 *in.*; *diameter* 9 *in.* COLL. *J.E.H.*

(No. 180.) A Circular Dish; decorated with flowers in the centre, surrounded by cornucopiæ and ornament, all in slight relief, and coloured in slip of rich brown tint on a buff glazed ground. Also initials in relief—

I.S.

Diameter $13\frac{3}{4}$ *in.* COLL. *T.B.*, LATE *W.E.*

(No. 181.) A small Puzzle Jug, with spout and perforations; very rich brown glaze, decorated with fine conventional design in yellow slip outlined with dots (yellow on a dark ground). A beautiful little piece.

I·B:

Height 5 *in.*; *diameter* 4 *in.* *B. MUS.* (*WILLETT COLL.*).

(No. 182.) A small, globular, One-handled Posset-Pot; yellow glaze, with florid decoration in brown slip. Inscribed with initials as part of the decoration—

S R

(No. 183.) A brown Bowl, on stand, with four handles and a whistle. Inscribed on outside edge with legend—

COM|GOOD|WEMAN|DRINK|OF|THE|
BEST| ON|MY|LADY|AND ALL THE
REST

Height 7 in.; diameter 8½ in. COLL. *LORD W.*

(No. 184.) A Puzzle Jug; rich brown glaze decorated with yellow slip spots, and inscribed with legend—

Gentlemen now try your Skill
ill hold you six-pence if you will
that you don't drink unless you spill.

Height 7 in.; diameter 5 in. COLL. *A.E.C.*

(No. 185.) A large Posset-Pot with three handles; black glaze, inscribed with legend in yellow slip. No decoration except the vertical, serrated, and twisted strips of same colour.

MARY:SMITH:
HER:CVP:

Height 7 in.; diameter 8 in.
B. Mus. (FRANKS COLL.).

(No. 186.) A Cradle; brilliant yellow glaze, decorated in rich brown slip with diagonal panelled ornament. The inscription is curious, and, had not Queen Mary been childless, it might have been supposed to have a reference to her. A large W occurs on one end of the cradle, and on the other an M, beneath which are two R's conjoined.

Height $6\frac{1}{8}$ *in.; length* $16\frac{1}{4}$ *in.* COLL. *J.E.H.*

(No. 187.) A Cylindrical Pot, originally with two handles, both of which are now unfortunately broken; yellow glaze, decorated with a good conventional design in very rich yellowish-brown slip, with dotted outline. The legend, in dotted letters, runs round the rim.

BRISK : BE : TO : THE : MED :
YOV : DESIER : AS : HER : LOVE :
YOV : MA : REQVIRE :

Height $5\frac{1}{4}$ *in.; diameter* $7\frac{1}{4}$ *in.* B. MUS. (WILLETT COLL.).

(No. 188.) A Piggin; yellow glaze, decorated with indented pattern in brown. Upright handle, bearing initials in brown slip. An almost identical specimen is in the Mayer Museum at Liverpool.

KS

Height $3\frac{1}{2}$ *in.; diameter* $4\frac{3}{4}$ *in.*
COLL. *M.P.G.*

(No. 189.) A Two-handled Posset-Pot, with cover; yellow glaze, decorated and inscribed in brown slip dotted with yellow—

THE·BEST·
IS·NOT·TOO·

Height 8 *in.; diameter* 6½ *in.*
B. Mus. (*Willett Coll.*).

(No. 190.) An octagonal Dish, decorated in a very uncommon style with pomegranates and fleur-de-lys. The raised outlines have been obtained with a graven mould, and the intervals filled in with slip. Inscribed with initials, probably of the maker's name—

2F

Diameter 13¼ *in.*
Coll. L.M.S.

(No. 191.) A very fine Dish; yellow glaze, decorated in brown slip in exactly the same style as the Toft dishes. A two-headed eagle occupies the field. Trellis border, inscribed with name.

Diameter 16½ *in.*
B. Mus. (*Willett Coll.*).

MARGERENASH

(No. 192.) **Metropolitan Slip.** A small Jug; brown glaze, decorated and inscribed in yellow slip. Found in Bishopsgate Street, 1884.

OBEAY THE KING

Height 5½ *in.; diameter* 4 *in.*
B. Mus. (*Franks Coll.*).

(No. 193.) **Metropolitan Slip.** A small Jug; brown glaze, decorated and inscribed in yellow slip. Found in Farringdon Street, 1880.

WHEN THIS YOU SEE REMEMBER ME
OBEAY GODS WOURD

Height 6¼ *in.; diameter* 5½ *in.* *B. Mus.* (*Franks Coll.*).

(No. 194.) **Metropolitan Slip.** A Pot, with handle broken; brown glaze, decorated and inscribed in yellow slip. Imperfect. Found in Newgate Street.

REMEMBER THY END TRVLY

Height 6 *in.; diameter* 7¼ *in.* *B. Mus.* (*Tylor Coll.*).

(No. 195.) **Metropolitan Slip.** A Pot, with one handle; of coarse ware with reddish-brown glaze, decorated in faint yellow slip, and inscribed in one line with decoration of stars and dashes below.

BE MERY AND WIE

Height 6½ *in.* *Coll. G. Mus.*

(No. 196.) **Metropolitan Slip.** A Cup, with handle, of the same coarse ware as No. 195; yellow slip on brown glaze. Slip decoration (wavy) on handle. Found in Railway Works betweeu Sun Street and Half-Moon Street, Bishopsgate, March, 1863.

Height $2\frac{1}{2}$ *in.; diameter* 4 *in.* COLL. G. MUS.

(No. 197.) **Metropolitan Slip.** A small Jug; brown glaze, inscribed in yellow slip. Found in Farringdon Street, 1880.

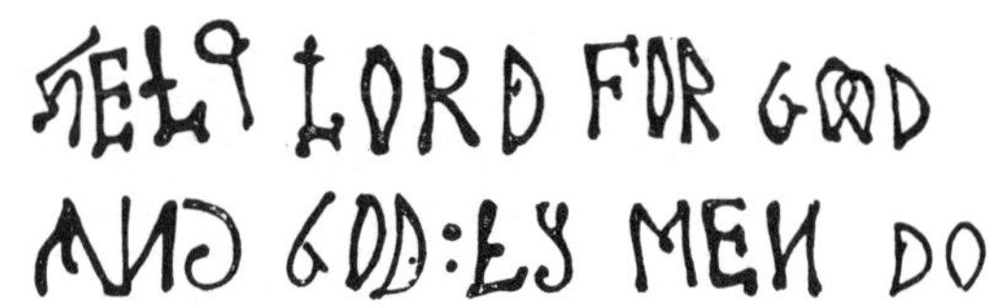

Height 6 *in.; diameter* $5\frac{3}{4}$ *in.*

B. Mus. (*Franks Coll.*).

(No. 198.) A Jug, closely resembling No. 147; yellow glaze, decorated in brown slip. The front is ornamented with a lion rampant on brown ground, and incised flowers. Inscribed with legend—

Despise me not because I'm made of clay
But make me wellcome when I come this way
my belly fill with Punch or good strong beer
and I will make you merry all the year.

Susannah Mason.

Height $10\frac{1}{2}$ *in.; diameter* $10\frac{1}{2}$ *in.* COLL. J.HA.

(No. 199.) A large Dish, of exactly the same character as the Toft dishes; brown glaze, decorated in yellow. A very bold figure of a cock occupies almost the whole field; a trumpet on the upper portion seems to furnish an allusion to the Cock and Trumpet, formerly a well-known inn-sign. Inscribed with initials and name—

HI
TOMKIS

Diameter $18\frac{3}{4}$ *in.*
COLL. *L. MUS.*

(No. 200.) A Three-handled Posset-Pot, mentioned by M. Solon, and ascribed by him to the collection of Mr. George T. Robinson. Inscribed with legend—

ROBART POOL MAD THIS CVP
WITH A GUD POSSET FIL AND

(No. 201.) A Two-handled Posset Pot, with lid, the latter imperfect. Yellow glaze over profuse embossed decoration of unusual character, and differing from Wrotham. Decoration in brown slip has also been applied, and the letters are in brown slip dotted with yellow. Inscribed with initials. A piece of very uncommon character.

AW

Height $12\frac{1}{4}$ *in.; diameter* $9\frac{1}{2}$ *in.*
COLL. *L. MUS.*

(No. 202.) A small Jug, with raised slip ornament of tulips, with rough scratched decoration and inscription. Probably of late date.

William
Cuttan

Diameter $3\frac{1}{2}$ *in.*
Coll. J.E.H.

(No. 203.) **Cock Pit Hill.** A Dish; yellow glaze, decorated in brown slip with yellow dots. The ornamentation consists of a tree with a single stem, from which spring two branches, with leaves, and three large flowers or suns. On each branch is perched a bird, probably intended for a cock. An oblong label in the centre is inscribed with initials, which may be those of the maker. Professor Church mentions a similar specimen as being in the collection of Mr. T. Kindale, and we have come across another specimen in Yorkshire.

Diameter 16 *in.* SM *B. Mus.* (*Willett Coll.*).

(No. 204.) **Cock Pit Hill.** A Dish, decorated in the centre with wyvern on human figure, border of royal badges, lion passant, and fleur-de-lys. Inscribed with initials—

Diameter $13\frac{1}{4}$ *in.* RS *B. Mus.* (*Willett Coll.*).

(No. 205.) **Cock Pit Hill.** A Dish, decorated with figure of St. George and the Dragon; yellow glaze, very rudely decorated in dark brown slip; with impressed inscription—

St George
Dragon
IB

Diameter 16 *in.* *B. Mus.* (*Franks Coll.*).

SGRAFIATO.

THE general characteristics of this ware resemble those of Slip-Decorated, the body being similar and the clays employed of nearly the same tones; but the decorative treatment is of quite a different kind. Where clays of two colours are employed on the same piece, the lighter is spread in a thin layer upon the darker, or *vice versâ*, and the ornamentation is obtained by removing the upper stratum in the desired pattern so as to disclose the lower. In many cases only one colour is employed, and the design or inscription is scratched in, just as occurs in the wares of Nottingham, Brampton, Chesterfield, etc., which find their place, however, under their respective headings.

This kind of ornament is found upon pieces of various shapes, including, amongst others, the *fuddling-cups*, intended for the discomfiture of the drinker, in which six or more pieces are so conjoined that all must be emptied at once.

A particularly interesting specimen of Sgrafiato Ware is No. 207, a plate in the possession of Dr. Norris, commemorating the same event as that to which allusion is made in the piece facsimiled in our frontispiece (viz., the birth of conjoined female twins), and supplying the date, 1680, which is wanting in the Lambeth Dish. The earliest date we record in this ware is 1670.

1670. (No. 206.) Bellied Jug; brown ware, streaked, highly glazed, bearing the date, two initials, and name on upper part, with a band round the centre; enclosed by incised dotted line, on which is inscription, also incised—

1670 John Wayman I F

COME BROTHER SHAL·

WE·IOYN·GIVE·ME YOUR·TWO

·PENCE·HERE IS IS MINE

Height 14 *in.; diameter* 12 *in.* COLL. N. MUS.

1680. (No. 207.) A Plate; of red pitcher clay, covered with a yellow glaze; containing a very rude device (which is simply drawn through the surface, showing an outline in red commemorating the birth of a double female child. In the centre is the representation of the child, red on a yellow ground, with date across the middle of their bodies, and the letters I O on one side of them and S D on the other. A rude, partially floral, decoration forms the side device. (*See* Note at end of volume, on No. 404, which commemorates the same event.)

Diameter 13¾ *in.* Coll. Dr. H.N.

1692. (No. 208.) A large Four-handled Goblet and Cover, possibly a christening-cup; of good shape, the sides ornamented with rough devices, impressed. Attached to one of the handles is a whistle. Inscription and date round rim. At the foot are the initials R K S K.

HERE I IS I THE I GEST I OF I THE I BARLY I KORNE I
GLAD I HAM I I THE I CILD I IS BORN 1692 IC RK SK

The initials I. G. may possibly refer to John Gauntlett of Amesbury, who, at the time, was making the celebrated Gauntlett tobacco-pipes from clay found at Chittom.

Coll. S. Mus.

1697. (No. 209.) A "Fuddling-Cup"; three cups conjoined in a triangular form, communicating with each other at the lowest part; with twisted handles. Inscribed, under the glaze, with legend and date. Yellow and green ware, highly glazed. A very beautiful little piece; probably made in the West of England, and of the same character as No. 221.

THREE MERY
BOYS 1697

Height 3 *in.; diameter* 5 *in.* COLL. T. MUS.

1703. (No. 210.) A large Jug, said to be of Devonshire manufacture, with one handle. Brown upon yellow, in heavy glaze. Decorated all round with a hunting scene—hounds, figures, and hare; bearing also initials and date. Inscription round the jug from top, but in no separate lines—

The fearfull Hare doth run apace.
Because the Honds are on thare chace.
The Country he is forst to fly
Whilst they are out with Hue and Cry.
Nature hath taught him in this strife
To seek for to preserve his life
Which he by running doth obtaine
And the Hounds retorne againe.
The Huntsman seeing that doth Cry
Lett him goe. his meat is dry.
I'll to my Landlady with speed
For i of her have greater need.

Height 12 *in.; diameter* 11 *in.* COLL. F.P.

1705. (No. 211.) A Christening-Cup, or "Gossips' Bowl," with three handles (one lost), whistle, and cover; of same shape and colour as No. 208; ornamented with floral devices and zigzag lines. Inscribed with legend, initials, and date—

WITH ALL MI HART I DRINK TO V
I WOLD HAVE BEERE BEFOR V GOO.
1705 . A . B . O . B

Coll. C.H.W.

1708. (No. 212.) A large globular Harvest-Jug; brown glaze, decorated in yellow with figures of a man and woman, birds and foliage. Inscription and date on heart in front of jug and round neck. Date quite clear, and occurs twice.

1708
It is cupid's
dart wound
ed my heart.

Lo i unto your house am ſent
as a token from a frind
When your harvest folks are dry
them i will there attend. 1708.

Height $13\frac{1}{2}$ *in.; diameter* 11 *in.*
B. Mus. (*Willett Coll.*).

1711. (No. 213.) A Christening-Cup, or "Gossips' Bowl," with four handles, whistle, and cover; of same shape and colour as Nos. 208 and 211. Inscribed with legend, initials, and date—

IF V LOVE ME LEND ME NOT
IF I HAM TOR I SHALL BE FORGOT.
1711 E H

Coll. C.H.W.

1726. (No. 214.) A Christening-Cup, or "Gossips' Bowl," with two handles, cover lost; of same shape and colour as Nos. 208, 211, and 213, ornamented with flowers and true lovers' knots. Inscribed with legend and date—

I DRINK TO YOU WITH ALL MV HART
MERY MET AND MERY PART. 1726

A similar Pot, with inscription but no date, is in Coll. C.H.W.

1730. (No. 215.) Six Cups conjoined, inscribed with legend and date—

fill me of sidful and drink . . . rs. Sp. Vm. maker
The gift is small. but good will is all. 1730.

Height $2\frac{3}{4}$ *in.; diameter* $8\frac{1}{4}$ *in.* B. MUS. (WILLETT COLL.).

1736. (No. 216.) A Triple Cup; inscribed with initials and date.

SM:EM
no the 22:1736

Height $2\frac{1}{4}$ *in.; diameter* $4\frac{1}{2}$ *in.*
B. MUS. (WILLETT COLL.).

1740. (No. 217.) A Basin; orange clay, covered with yellow slip and decorated in Sgrafiato with rough figures of a bird and flower. Inscribed with date. *Height* $3\frac{1}{2}$ *in.; diameter* $5\frac{1}{2}$ *in.*

1752. (No. 218.) Six Cups conjoined, similar to Nos. 209 and 215; inscribed under the glaze with legend, date, and initials—

Fill me for your Ease
Drink what you please
1752. *F.N.*

Height $2\frac{1}{2}$ *in.; diameter* 6 *in.*

1755. (No. 219.) A Bowl; body brown; inside cream-coloured; washed with slip of Devon clay, and ornamented with rudely incised figures of lions and fishes, scratched through with a style so as to expose the body, and then glazed. Inscribed with date—

1755

Height 4 *in.; diameter* $9\frac{1}{4}$ *in.*

COLL. *M.P.G.*

1764. (No. 220.) A Two-handled Posset-Pot; body brown; covered on the outside with cream-coloured slip, which has been cut through in horizontal lines and vertical bands, and then roughly decorated in a blue pattern. The whole of fine clay, well potted, and highly glazed. Inscribed with initials and date—

SL 1764

Height 8 *in.; diameter* 10 *in.* COLL. *J.E.H.*

1766. (No. 221.) A Jug; brown body; marbled ware. Inscribed with name and date—

John & Dorothy Cook. 1766

Height $10\frac{1}{8}$ *in.; diameter* $6\frac{1}{2}$ *in.* COLL. *A.E.C.*

1766. (No. 222.) A "Fuddling-Cup"; six cups arranged in a triangular form, communicating with each other at the lowest part, with twisted bands surrounding them on the outside; three handles; yellow and green ware, highly glazed. Inscription under the glaze—

Fill this Cup and
Drink it up.
S 1766

Height $2\frac{3}{4}$ *in.; diameter* $7\frac{3}{4}$ *in.*
COLL. *J.E.H.*

1770. (No. 223.) Six Cups conjoined; a similar specimen to No. 222. Inscribed with legend, initials, and date—

My frend is He That loue me well
But Ho he is I cannot tell. I.M. 1770.

Height 3 *in; diameter* 7 *in.* *B. Mus.* (*Willett Coll.*).

1779. (No. 224.) A Jug; body of marble ware in two shades of brown (made of mixed clays), partly covered with cream-coloured slip, cut through to the ground in four ornamented bands and floral decoration. Inscribed—

George Benteley 1779
Fill us the Other Jug ⁂

Height 10 *in.; diameter* 7 *in.* COLL. *J.E.H.*

1781. (No. 225.) A Money-Box; cream-coloured ground, decorated in brown. On the top a hen and eight chickens, one on her back. A slit in front in shape of a cross (broken away), below name and date—

Thomas Leaher

1781.

Height $3\frac{3}{4}$ *in.; diameter* 4 *in.*

1791. (No. 226.) A Two-handled Jar and Cover. Inscribed with legend and date—

I am But Small for Sugers Dear
of it Be Sure that you take care. Molley Saveall. 1791.

Height 8 *in.; diameter* 6 *in.* *B. Mus.* (*Willett Coll.*).

SGRAFIATO, UNDATED.

(No. 227.) A Jug; of common brick clay, coated with yellow slip, which has been scraped off so as to form a decoration. In front is the sun, on one side a bird and flowers, and on the other an inscription. The date was obliterated by the person herself for whom the jug was made, as when she became old she did not like to have her age so recorded.

Come Fill me Full with Liquor Sweet
For that is good when Friends do meet,
But pray take care don't let me fall
Least you list your liquor jug and all.

Catherine Davies aged 8 *years.*

Height $8\frac{1}{2}$ *in.* *Coll. L.M.S.*

(No. 228.) A small Jug, with one handle; high glaze over green and brown colouring. Decorated in front with the Arms of England, the Lion and the Unicorn supporters, and "Honi soit qui maley pence" written between. Inscription on back—

As A ring is round
And hath no end
So is my love
Unto my
friend

Height 6½ *in.; diameter* 5 *in.* COLL. F.P.

LAMBETH DELFT.

THE body of this ware is of a pale buff tint, considerably harder, and less friable, whilst the enamel is whiter, more opaque, and much "softer" looking than that of the Dutch Delft with which we are so familiar. It differs from the Delft of Bristol and Liverpool in tone, glaze, and decoration; the lettering is, as will be seen by the facsimiles, quite *sui generis*, and very characteristic. The tone of the blue decoration is also, as a rule, much paler or greyer than that of other English Delft. It occurs in a variety of forms: plates, dishes, cups, mugs (only one jug of ordinary shape has come under our notice), drug-pots, candlesticks, pill-slabs, and notably in that of wine-jars, peculiar (with one exception, *possibly* a Bristol vessel) to this ware. The earliest date with which we are acquainted occurs on a mug in the Museum of Practical Geology, 1631–32 (No. 229), the earliest wine-jar being dated 1640, and the latest 1672. The most interesting specimen in this ware which we have come across is that which stands as the frontispiece to this volume, a full history of which will be found in our note at the end of the book.

Except where mention is made to the contrary, all the under-mentioned pieces of Lambeth Delft have a surface of white enamel, highly glazed, and are decorated in blue.

1631. (No. 229.) A barrel-shaped Mug, with one handle; decorated in
1632. blue with birds, insects, and flowers. Inscribed on a band round the rim with legend and date. Dated also with a date of a year later under the handle.

WILLIAM AND
ELIZABETH BVRGES:
24TH AVGVST 1631 1632

Height 6½ in. Coll. M.P.G.

1633. (No. 230.) Three Vases, conjoined; with twisted handles. Inscribed with initials and date—

I.S. 1633

Height 3¼ *in.* COLL. *J.F.*

1634. (No. 231.) A barrel-shaped Mug, with one handle; similar to No. 229. Inscribed with name and date on band, with ornaments above and below—

IOHN∴LEMAN

1634

Height 5 *in.; diameter* 3¾ *in.* *B. Mus.* (*Willett Coll.*).

1636. (No. 232.) A round Dish; ornamented round the edge, in panels, with designs in blue. In the centre blue medallion (supported by a lion and a leopard), on which is placed an ornamented shield inscribed with initials and date—

E. B.

1636

Diameter 16 *in.* COLL. LORD *W.*

1640. (No. 233.) A Wine-Jar; inscribed in front with name and date—

W:YORKE

16 40

Height 6⅛ *in.* *B. Mus.* (*Franks Coll.*).

This is the earliest date we find recorded on vessels of this description.

1641. (No. 234.) A Wine-Jar; inscribed with name and date—

WHIT

1641

COLL. LATE *R.H.S.-S.*

1641. (No. 235.) A Wine-Jar, decorated in blue and a little yellow. Inscribed with name, initials, and date—

RENISH WINE
S
I E
1641

Height 6 *in.*
B. Mus. (*Franks Coll.*).

1641. (No. 236.) A Wine-Jar; inscribed with name and date—

WHIT WINE

Height 6¾ *in.* 1641 *S. K. Mus.* (*Schreiber Coll.*).

1641. (No. 237.) A semicircular Cistern; inscription on front, date on back.

G ◦ F ◦ 1641 *Height* 8 *in; diameter* 7 *in.*
B. Mus. (*Willett Coll.*).

1642. (No. 238.) A large Dish, decorated in blue, rather in Japanese style, with ships, a windmill, and pagodas. Coat of arms in the centre; also initials, date, and name "The Clarkes," on a band or scroll below. *Coll. H.W.*

M
R A
ANNO DOM
16 42

1642. (No. 239.) A Wine-Jar; inscribed with name and date—

CLARET
1642

Yniscedwyn House, Swansea.

1642. (No. 240.) A bowl-shaped Mug, with one handle, rudely painted in imitation of Majolica ware with arabesques in blue and yellow. Inscription on band round the rim—

ANN ◇ CHAPMAN ◇
ANNO ◇ 1642

Height 5 *in.*; *diameter* 4½ *in.*
COLL. *S. K. Mus.*

1642. (No. 241.) A Wine-Jar; inscribed with name and date—

WHIT
1642

1643. (No. 242.) A Wine-Jar; inscribed with name and date—

WHIT
1643

Height 7 *in.*; *diameter* 5 *in.*
COLL. *Capt. M.*

1643. (No. 243.) A Wine-Jar; inscribed with name and date as above, but of smaller dimensions.

Height 5¾ *in.*; *diameter* 4 *in.* COLL. *T. Mus.*

1643. (No. 244.) A Wine-Jar; inscribed below handle with name and date—

SACK
1643

Height 6¼ *in.*
COLL. *Earl Mt. E.*

1643. (No. 245.) A Wine-Jar; inscribed with name and date—

Height $6\frac{1}{4}$ *in.; diameter* 5 *in.*

COLL. *J.E.H.*

1644. (No. 246.) A Wine-Jar; inscribed with name and date—

Height $6\frac{1}{2}$ *in.; diameter* $4\frac{3}{8}$ *in.*

COLL. DR. *J.E.*

1644. (No. 247.) A Wine-Jar; inscribed with name and date—

Height $6\frac{1}{4}$ *in.; diameter* $4\frac{1}{2}$ *in.*

COLL. DR. *J.E.*

1644. (No. 248.) A Wine-Jar; inscribed with initials, encircled with a wreath, and date below—

Height $7\frac{1}{2}$ *in.*

COLL. *Y. MUS.*

1645. (No. 249.) A Wine-Jar; inscribed with name and date—

SACK 1645

Height $8\frac{1}{4}$ *in.* COLL. LATE *R.H.S.-S.*; *also* COLL. CAPT. *M.*

1645. (No. 250.) A Barrel-shaped Mug, with one handle; similar to No. 240. Decorated in blue with ships and landscape. Inscribed with name and date on a scroll round the rim—

Coll. Mayer Mus.

1645. (No. 251.) A Wine-Jar; inscribed with name and date—

Height $7\frac{1}{2}$ *in.; diameter* $5\frac{1}{4}$ *in.*
B. Mus. (*Franks Coll.*).

1646. (No. 252.) A Wine-Jar; inscribed with name and date—

Height $5\frac{3}{4}$ *in.*
Schreiber Coll.; also H.G.

1646. (No. 253.) A Wine-Jar; inscribed with name and date—

Height $4\frac{3}{4}$ *in.; diameter* $3\frac{1}{4}$ *in.*
Coll. Dr. E.;
also Earl of Mt. E.

1647. (No. 254.) A Wine-Jar; inscribed with name and date; handle broken.

Height $6\frac{1}{2}$ *in.*
Coll. M.P.G.

1647. (No. 255.) A Wine-Jar; inscribed with initials, name, and date. Originally in the Strawberry Hill Collection.

Height $6\frac{5}{8}$ *in.*

Coll. Gen. P.R., late W.E.

1647. (No. 256.) A Wine-Jar; inscribed with names and date, and decorated with a coat of arms—

Height $6\frac{1}{4}$ *in.; diameter* $4\frac{1}{2}$ *in.*

Coll. J.E.H.

1647. (No. 257.) A Wine-Jar; inscribed with names and date. An exactly similar specimen to above. Obtained from a Mr. Williamson, who inherited it, it having belonged to an uncle of his grandfather, whose name was Allen, and a lineal descendant of the Wm. Allen on the Jug, and of Buckinghamshire family.

Height $5\frac{3}{4}$ *in.; diameter* $4\frac{1}{2}$ *in. B. Mus. (Franks Coll.).*

1647. (No. 258.) A Wine-Jar; inscribed with name and date—

SACK · 1647

Coll. H.W.;
also Fortnum Coll.

1647. (No. 259.) A Wine-Jar; inscribed with name and date—

Height $4\frac{3}{4}$ *in.*
S. K. Mus. (*Schreiber Coll.*).

1648. (No. 260.) A Wine-Jar; inscribed with name and date—

WHIT
1648

Height $6\frac{3}{4}$ *in.; diameter* $4\frac{3}{4}$ *in.*
Coll. Norwich Mus.

1648. (No. 261.) A Wine-Jar; inscribed with name and date—

Height $4\frac{3}{4}$ *in.; diameter* $3\frac{1}{2}$ *in.*
B. Mus. (*Franks Coll.*);
also Coll. J.E.H.

1648. (No. 262.) A Wine-Jar; inscribed with name and date—

CLARET
1648

Height 6 *in.; diameter* $4\frac{1}{2}$ *in.*
Coll. N. Mus.

1648. (No. 263.) A Bowl; inscribed with initials and date—

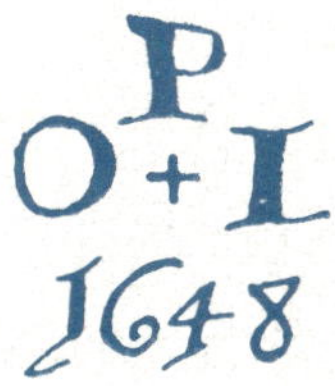

Height $2\frac{1}{2}$ *in.; diameter* 12 *in.*
Coll. H.W.

1648. (No. 264.) A Candlestick, coated with an opaque white tin enamel, painted in blue with the arms of the Fishmongers' Company, and inscribed with initials and date—

Height 10½ *in.*

COLL. *M.P.G.*

1649. (No. 265.) A Posset-Pot and Cover; decorated with the arms of the Grocers' Company in a scrolled shield on one side of the spout, and initials and date enclosed in crossed branches on the other side.

Height 9 *in.; diameter* 6⅛ *in.*

COLL. *D. Mus.*

1649. (No. 266.) A Wine-Jar; inscribed with initials and date, and decorated with a coat of arms. This bottle was found at Norwich, and was doubtless made for Edward Woodward, whose Token will be found described in Boyne (Norfolk, No. 183). He was a grocer, and seems to have anticipated a modern enactment in adding the trade of vintner to his original occupation. An exactly similar specimen is in the Norwich Museum.

Height 7¾ *in.;*
diameter 6 *in.*

COLL. *J.E.H.*

1649. (No. 267.) A Wine-Jar; inscribed with name and date—

SACK

1649

Coll. L.M.S.

1649. (No. 268.) A Wine-Jar; inscribed with name and date—

Height $4\frac{1}{2}$ *in.; diameter* 4 *in.*

Coll. J.E.H.

1649. (No. 269.) A Wine-Jar; inscribed with name and date—

Height 6 *in.; diameter* $4\frac{1}{4}$ *in.*

B. Mus. (Franks Coll.);

also Coll. Gen. P.R., late W.E. Height $5\frac{3}{4}$ *in.;*

also Coll. H.W.

1650. (No. 270.) A Wine-Jar; inscribed with name and date—

Height 6 *in.*

Coll. J.F.

1650. (No. 271.) A very fine Wine-Jar; decorated in front with a shield containing the arms of the family for whom it was made. Inscribed with names and date. A very interesting and unusual specimen.

1650

IOHN:SMITH

AND:MARGERI

Height $7\frac{1}{4}$ in. *Coll. B. Mus.* (*late W.E.*).

1650. (No. 272.) A Wine-Jar; inscribed with name and date—

SACK

1650

Height $5\frac{3}{4}$ in.; diameter $4\frac{1}{2}$ in. *Coll. J.E.H.*

Height $7\frac{1}{4}$ in. *Coll. late W.E.; and Coll. N. Mus.*

Height $4\frac{1}{2}$ in.; diameter $3\frac{1}{2}$ in. *B. Mus.* (*Willett Coll.*).

Height 6 in. *Coll. Y. Mus.*

1650. (No. 273.) A Wine-Jar; inscribed with name and date—

CLARET

1650

Height $8\frac{1}{8}$ in. *Coll. L. Mus.*

1650. (No. 274.) A Wine-Jar; inscribed as above. This specimen was found in an old house which was being demolished at Shifnal, Shropshire, about thirty years ago.

Coll. W.C.

1650. (No. 275.) A Chalice-shaped Cup; decorated in blue and yellow with device of eagle and child. Inscribed, in blue, with name and date—

WILLIAM LAMBOTh

1650

Height 4½ *in.; diameter* 3¾ *in.*
B. Mus. (*Willett Coll.*).

1651. (No. 276.) A Wine-Jar; inscribed with name and date—

SACK

1651

Coll. W.C. and J.B.

1651. (No. 277.) A Wine-Jar; inscribed with name and date—

CLARET

1651

Height 8 *in.; diameter* 5¾ *in.*
B. Mus. (*Franks Coll.*), *and Coll. H.W.*

1651. (No. 278.) A Two-handled Posset-Pot, with cover. Decorated in the centre of one side with initials and date, enclosed within a border of foliage, forming a medallion, with a Royal Crown above and a mark below. The date occurs again inside the cover. A rare and perfect specimen. (*See* Note at end of volume.)

K·G
1651

Height 7 *in.; diameter* 7 *in.*
Coll. J.E.H., late W.E.

1652. (No. 279.) A Wine-Jar; inscribed with initials, name, and date—

Height 7 *in.*
B. Mus. (*Willett Coll.*).

1652. (No. 280.) A Wine-Jar; inscribed with name and date—

Height $5\frac{3}{4}$ *in.*
Coll. late W.E.
Height $6\frac{1}{2}$ *in.*
Coll. Dr. J.E.
Height 5 *in.*
Coll. Capt. M., and H. Mus.

1652. (No. 281.) A Drug-Pot; cylindrical; inscription and date on framed panel—

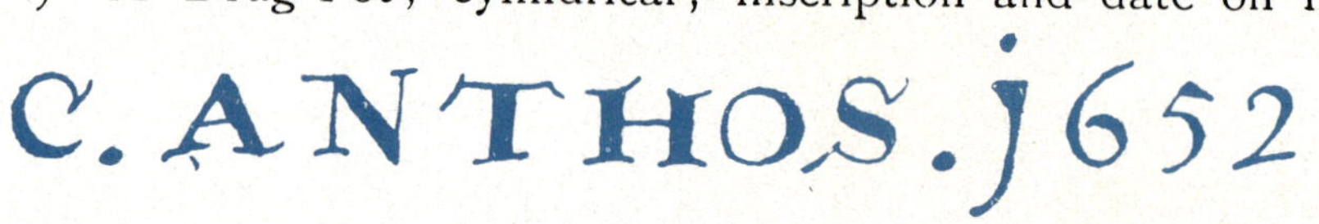

Height $5\frac{3}{4}$ *in.* *B. Mus.* (*Franks Coll.*).

1653. (No. 282.) A large Dish; coarse body, coated with a dull glaze, and painted in blue, green, yellow, orange, and purple. Subject—Christ and His disciples on the road to Emmaus; above the figure of Christ a bird, symbolising the Holy Spirit, and in the clouds the word GOD. Dated in blue on quatrefoil in foreground—

Diameter $14\frac{1}{2}$ *in.* *Coll. M.P.G.*

1653. (No. 283.) A fine Dish, with lobed sides; the whole surface of the centre decorated in blue and yellow with the arms, crest, helmet, and mantling of the Packer Family, of Essex. Inscribed with initials and date—

A P M
16 53

Diameter 11 *in.*
COLL. *B. Mus.*, LATE *W.E.*

1653. (No. 284.) A Wine-Jar; inscribed with name and date—

CLARET
1653

Height 8 *in.; diameter* 5 *in.*
B. Mus. (WILLETT COLL.).

1654. (No. 285.) A large Dish; coated with white enamel, and painted in blackish blue with the arms of the City of London. Inscription and date. The dish has been broken and riveted.

AN.. NO...
16 54
LONDE....

Diameter $15\frac{1}{4}$ *in.* COLL. *M.P.G.*

1655. (No. 286.) A small Wine-Jar; inscribed with legend and date—

DRINKE : AND : BE : MERY : 1655

Exhibited by Mrs. Newton at the Royal Archæological Institute, 1879.

1655. (No. 287.) A large Dish; the edge and central ornament surrounding the boss, on which the arms of the Pewterers' Company are painted, are moulded in relief. Inscribed with initials and date—

Diameter 16½ *in.*

COLL. B. MUS.

1655. (No. 288.) A Wine-Jar; inscribed with initials and date—

Height 6 *in.*

COLL. LATE W.E.

1655. (No. 289.) A Cup, on foot; inscribed with name and date—

Mary Butler. 1655.

COLL. H.G.

1656. (No. 290.) A Wine-Jar; inscribed with name and date—

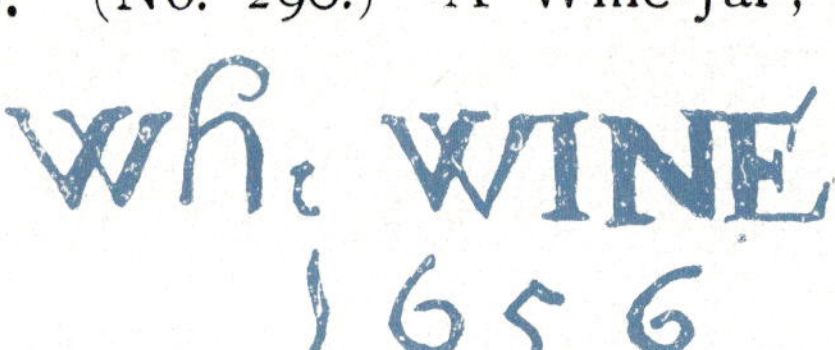

Height 4½ *in.; diameter* 3¾ *in.*

B. MUS. (WILLETT COLL.).

1656. (No. 291.) A Wine-Jar; inscribed with name and date—

WHIT
1656

Coll. H.W. and H.G.

1656. (No. 292.) A Wine-Jar; inscribed with name and date—

SACK
1656

B. Mus. (Willett Coll.).

1657. (No. 293.) A Wine-Jar; inscribed with initials, name, and date—

M·P
SACK
1657

Height $5\frac{1}{2}$ *in.*
B. Mus. (Franks Coll.).

1657. (No. 294.) A small Posset-Pot, with handle; white glaze, decorated in blue and yellow with Bakers' arms. Inscribed with legend, also with initials and date, which occur in two places. Inside is painted a rabbit.

·DRINKE·VP·: YOVR: DRINKE

A M R 1657

Height $3\frac{1}{4}$ *in.; diameter* $4\frac{1}{4}$ *in.*
Coll. J.E.H.

1657. (No. 295.) A Two-handled Posset-Pot, with spout; inscribed with initials and date—

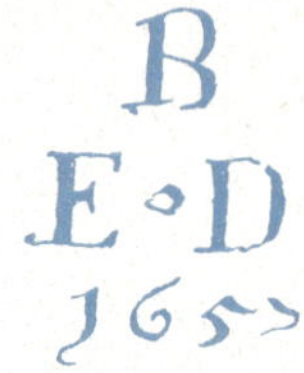

Height 5 *in.; diameter* 6½ *in.*
B. Mus. (*Willett Coll.*).

1657. (No. 296.) A large Dish, with fine border; decorated in the centre with drinking scene, and inscribed with initials and date—

Diameter 19⅛ *in.*
Coll. L. Mus.

1658. (No 297.) A Posset-Pot, with one handle; white glaze, somewhat over-fired. Inscribed with name, initials, and date—

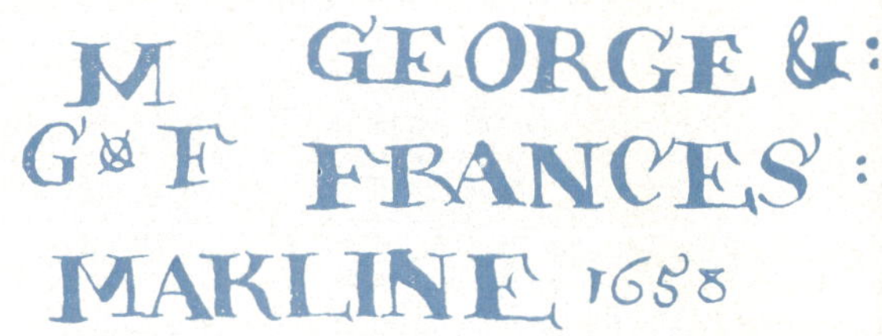

Height 4 *in.; diameter* 4½ *in.* *Coll. J.E.H.*

1658. (No. 298.) A Flower-Vase, in the shape of a book; inscribed with initials and date on both sides, enclosed in the form of a heart.

Height 4 *in.*
B. Mus. (*Willett Coll.*)

1658. (No. 299.) A Jug, with foot lost; inscribed in front with initials and date—

B
T I
1658

Present height $5\frac{3}{4}$ *in.*

COLL. — *D.*

1659. (No. 300.) A cylindrical Mug, decorated in blue; in the centre a shield with arms of the Carpenters' Company; within, an ornamental border of scroll-work and foliage. Inscribed with initials and date—

S
H P
1659

Height 5 *in.; diameter* $3\frac{1}{2}$ *in.*

COLL. LATE *W.E.*

1659. (No. 301.) "A Bottle of Sack, inscribed, was found by some labourers, in August, 1735, whilst draining a fish-pond at Hempstead, Herts, embedded in mud at least three feet deep. The mouth of the bottle was waxed over, and the wine perfectly good when tasted; but decay had nearly destroyed the cork." The inscription was as follows—

New Canary put in to see long keep good.
April 1659. *Ri. Combe.*

Extract from Descriptive Catalogue of the London Traders' Tavern and Coffee-House Tokens of the 16th Century, p. 228.

1659. (No. 302.) A Wine-Jar; inscribed with name and date; mentioned by Mr. Marryatt as belonging to Hon. R. Curzon, Jun.

SACK 1659

1659. (No. 303.) A large oval Dish, evidently copied from Palissy, representing Venus and Cupids. The figures are in relief. The border is sunk into four oval and four circular depressions; in the ovals are the seasons personified, in the circulars appear initials, the arms of the City of London, the date and the arms of the Pewterers' Company, all painted in blue, yellow, and green. (*See* Nos. 374 and 423 for similar specimens.) A similar specimen, 19 in. long, in the Hailstone Collection, is now in possession of Mr. Thomas Boynton.

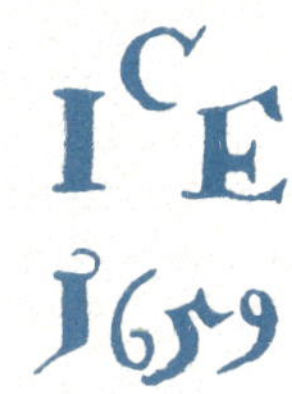

Length 17 *in.* *B. Mus.* (*Bernal Coll.*).

1659. (No. 304.) A Dish; painted in blue, yellow, green, and maroon; back yellow. Subject: The Prodigal Son. Border decorated with grotesques. (Same style as No. 309 in B. Mus. Coll.)

Inscribed on front

on back

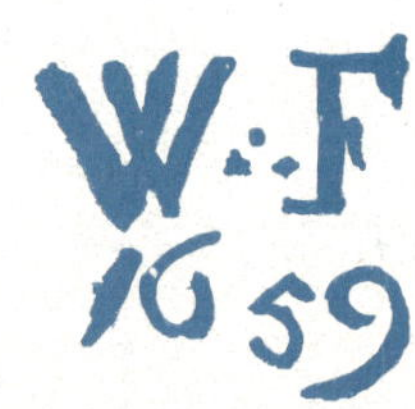

Diameter 20 *in.* *B. Mus.* (*Franks Coll.*).

1660. (No. 305.) A Drug-Pot, with spout and handle. Inscription on ribbon, angel's head above. Inscribed also with initials and date—

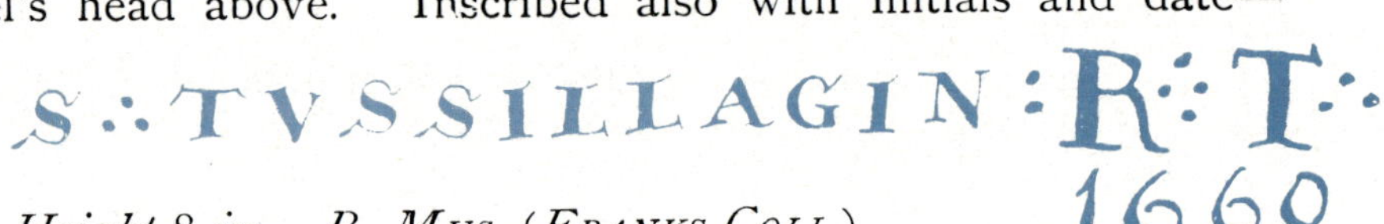

Height 8 *in.* *B. Mus.* (*Franks Coll.*).

1660. (No. 306.) A Posset-Pot, with one handle; decorated with the arms of the Leathersellers' Company, over which are initials I D I. Inscription and date round the rim—

BEE MERRY AND WISE 1660

Height 4¼ *in.; diameter* 4 *in.* B. MUS. (FRANKS COLL.).

1660. (No. 307.) A small Dish, with scalloped and fluted edge; inscribed with initials and date—

T T A
1660

Diameter 9 *in.*
COLL. MRS. P.

1660. (No. 308.) A Drug-Pot; decorated with initials and date in a shield bordered and shaded in blue with buff mantlings.

B
T D
1660

Height 6¾ *in.; diameter* 4⅞ *in.*
COLL. DR. J.E.

1660. (No. 309.) A circular Dish, painted in blue, yellow, and green. In the centre Jacob's dream is represented. Broad border, with four medallions decorated with the seasons, divided by rich Renaissance ornaments of animal forms. Inscribed with initials and date—

GENESIS The 28
CH 1660

Diameter 16 *in.*
COLL. *B. Mus.*

1660. (No. 310.) A large Dish, moulded; inscribed, on shield, with initials and date—

R
NA
1660

COLL. LORD *S.*

1661. (No. 311.) A Plate, octagonal in form; sunk octagonal centre; white glaze; no ornament except the flourished writing in blue.

Diameter, across corners, 8¼ *in.* COLL. *J.E.H.*

1661. (No. 312.) A deep Plate; white glaze, no ornament, inscription in blue—

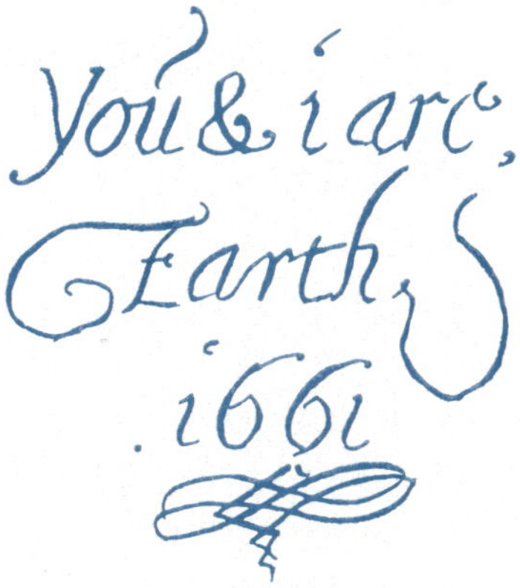

Diameter $8\frac{1}{4}$ *in.*
Coll. J.E.H.

1662. (No. 313.) A Wine-Jar; inscribed with name and date—

Height $6\frac{1}{2}$ *in.* *Coll. M.P.G.;*
also B. Mus. (*Franks Coll.*).

1662. (No. 314.) A Cup; with an inscription and date under a crown—

Height $2\frac{3}{4}$ *in; diameter* $3\frac{1}{4}$ *in.*
Coll. H.W.

M. Solon mentions a similar example as being in the collection of Prof. Church.

1662. (No. 315.) A Posset-Pot, with one handle; brilliant white glaze, and good decoration in Chinese taste; two sitting figures. Inscribed with initials and date. A very pretty specimen.

Height 4¼ *in.; diameter* 4¾ *in.* Coll. *J.E.H.*

1663. (No. 316.) A Wine-Jar; inscribed with name and date. Mentioned by Prof. Church.

CLARET
1663

1663. (No. 317.) A small Wine-Jar; inscribed with date.

Coll. *H.G.*

1663. (No. 318.) A Flower-Vase, in form of a book; the clasps gone. White glaze, decorated in blue with fleurs-de-lys in corners of the covers. Date in a lozenge, foliated.

Height 5 *in.; diameter* 3¼ *in.* Coll. *J. Ha.*

1663. (No. 319.) A very large Dish; decorated in blue, green, and yellow. In the centre a coat of arms, initials, and date, in blue, surmounted with a crown in green and yellow.

Diameter 15¾ *in.* Coll. *H.W.*

1664. (No. 320.) A large, deep Dish, fluted in large lobes; decorated with medallion enclosing initials and date—

* M *
G * P
1664

Diameter 13¼ *in.*
COLL. — *D.*

1666. (No. 321.) A Drug-Pot; white glaze, with blue decoration of the usual kind, viz., an angel's head and wings surmounting a scroll with divided ends, upon which is inscription and date—

:S: PŒNIÆ: 3ii:

1666

Height 6⅜ *in.*; *diameter* 5½ *in.*
COLL. *J.E.H.*

1666. (No. 322.) An oval, fluted Tray, with two handles; inscribed in the centre with initials and date—

S·H
1666

Length 7½ *in.*
B. Mus. (*Franks Coll.*).

1666. (No. 323.) A Cup, with a handle; inscribed with initials and date—

II CR D/2 1666

Height 2¾ *in.*;
diameter 3¼ *in.*
COLL. *H.W.*

1667. (No. 324.) A small Mug, with a twisted handle; decorated in blue, and inscribed with initials and date—

R
A I
1667

Coll. L.M.S.

1668. (No. 325.) A Drug-Pot, with inscription and date—

LEPVLM . VVLP . 1668

Height $7\frac{3}{4}$ *in.; diameter* $5\frac{3}{8}$ *in.* *Coll. Dr. J.E.*

1668. (No. 326.) A Jug, of very uncommon shape in this ware; very soft white enamel; decorated in rather deeper blue than usual. The ornament is like that of No. 315, page 88, which it much resembles, and is distinctly suggestive of Oriental inspiration.

Height 7 *in.; diameter* 5 *in.* *Coll. J.H.*

1670. (No. 327.) A large, deep Dish, with very broad lobes; decorated with a medallion enclosing initials and date—

Diameter $17\frac{1}{4}$ *in.*

Coll. — D.

1670. (No. 328.) A Cup, with one handle; white glaze, decorated in blue with arms of the Carpenters' Company. Inscribed with initials and date—

Height 5¼ *in.; diameter* 3⅝ *in.* COLL. D. MUS.

1671. (No. 329.) A Drug-Pot; with inscription, initials, and date—

LIN. ARCEI :· B.B 1671

Height 7¼ *in.; diameter* 5¼ *in.* COLL. Y. MUS.

1671. (No. 330.) A Dish; decorated in Majolica colours, green, blue, and yellow; a coat of arms in the centre, inscribed above with date—

1671 *Diameter* 13¼ *in.* COLL. L. MUS.

1671. (No. 331.) A Plate; decorated in blue with Chinese figures. Inscribed with initials and date—

Diameter 8¼ *in.* COLL. B. MUS.

W
G · S
1671

1672. (No. 332.) A Wine-Jar; decorated with the arms of Hunlock in blue and yellow. Inscribed with initial and date below the handle. An exactly similar specimen was in the collection of the late Mr. Soden-Smith. This date is the latest hitherto recorded on such vessels.

W
1672

Height 6½ *in.* B. MUS. (FRANKS COLL.)

1672. (No. 333.) A Drug-Pot; with inscription and date—

CIT· DECORT·1672 *Coll. H.W.*

1672. (No. 334.) A Vessel in the shape of a Cat, seated; painted in blue, inscribed with initials and date. Similar to No. 337, in British Museum.

S
R·I
1672

Height 6½ *in.*
Coll. H.W.

1673. (No. 335.) A Drug-Pot; with inscription, initials, and date—

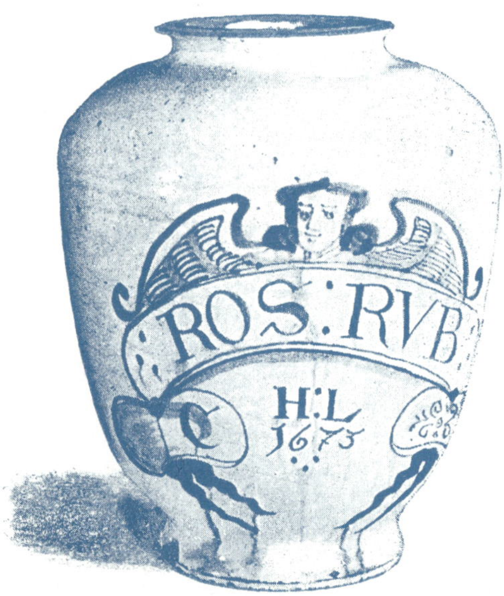

·:ROS:RVB:·

H:L
1673

Height 10½ *in.*
Coll. J.E.H.

1673. (No. 336.) A Dish or Strainer, with two handles, and six rows of perforations in concentric circles, painted in pale blue. Inscribed with initials and date on the reverse—

V
HM
1673

Diameter 13¾ *in.*
Coll. M.P.G.

1674. (No. 337.) A Vessel in the shape of a Cat, seated; painted in blue and yellow, and inscribed on its breast with initials and date. A similar specimen to No. 334, in the collection of Mr. Willett.

Height 6½ *in.*
B. Mus. (*Willett Coll.*).

1674. (No. 338.) A very fine circular Dish; decorated in bright blue, with the arms of England in the centre; on base supporting them, inscription and date; in field, initials; the broad border decorated with seven medallions, of which the top one bears a half-length portrait of King and initials C.R.; in four others are represented human heads, one with a scroll issuing from the mouth; in the other two, birds are depicted.

Diameter 19 *in.*
B. Mus. (*Willett Coll.*).

1674. (No. 339.) A Drug-Pot, decorated in the usual style; inscription and date on scroll under spout.

Height 6½ *in.*; *diameter* 5½ *in.*
Coll. T.B.

1674. (No. 340.) A Drug-Pot, similar to No. 339, with inscription and date—

+S:RHÆDOS:1674

Height 6½ *in.; diameter* 5½ *in.* COLL. *T.B.*

1674. (No. 341.) A standing Puzzle-Cup; open-work edge; syphon in centre; decorated with arms of Mercers' Company, and inscribed with initials and date. A beautiful and uncommon specimen. The taste displayed in this vessel is much in advance of that usually found in English pottery of this period.

I·W 1674

Height 9½ *in.*
B. Mus. (*Frank's Coll.*).

1675. (No. 342.) A Puzzle-Jug; inscribed with initials and date—

16 WC 75

Height 7⅜ *in.; diameter* 4¼ *in.* COLL. *M.P.G.*

1676. (No. 343.) A Drinking-Vessel in the shape of a Cat; in front, a heart-shaped medallion inscribed with initials and date—

L
TM
1676

Height 6⅜ *in.*
S. K. Mus. (*Schreiber Coll.*).

1679. (No. 344.) A six-sided Basket, with open-work sides; inscribed inside, in the centre, with initials and date—

M·:·T
1679

Height 4 *in.; diameter* 13 *in.*
B. Mus. (*Franks Coll.*).

1680. (No. 345.) A Drug-Pot, of the usual character; with inscription, initials, and date—

V:MARTIATV T·W
1680

Height 6 *in. B. Mus.* (*Willett Coll.*).

1680. (No. 346.) A Bowl; decorated with coat of arms, and inscribed with initials and date—

L
16 RK 80

Height $5\frac{1}{2}$ *in.; diameter* $15\frac{3}{4}$ *in.*
Coll. H.W.

1682. (No. 347.) A Plate; inscribed with initials and date—

S.B. 1682

Diameter $8\frac{5}{8}$ *in. M. Mus.*

1682. (No. 348.) A Plate; decorated with a portrait of Queen Catharine of Braganza, wife of Charles II.; with inscription painted in blue and yellow. Mentioned by Chaffers.

K 2 R 1682

1682. (No. 349.) A Mug; of a pale bluish green, decorated in blue with Fishmongers' arms, and inscribed with initials and date—

W
I S 1682

Height 5 *in.; diameter* 5 *in.*
Coll. H.W.

1684. (No. 350.) A circular Plate; decorated in the centre with an inscription beneath a crown supported by dragons. Inscribed on rim with initials and date—

what is a
merrey man
I C S
1684

Coll. Mayer Mus.

This Plate is one of a series of six. (*See* Nos. 394, 398, 399, 400, 401 for similar specimens and continuation of legend.)

1684. (No. 351.) A Drug-Pot; with inscription, initials, and date—

METHRIDAT
M:H
1684

Height $7\frac{3}{4}$ *in.; diameter* 6 *in.*

Coll. J.H.

1684. (No. 352.) A Puzzle-Pot, with false bottom enclosing a cavity which communicates with three tubular handles; coarsely painted in blue in oriental style, and inscribed with initials and date—

C
T:E
1684

Coll. M.P.G.

1684. (No. 353.) A small circular Plate; decorated with Chinese figures, and inscribed with initials and date—

R.C
1684

Coll. H.G.

1686. (No. 354.) An octagonal Plate; inscribed with initials and date—

M · S
1686

Coll. H.G.

1687. (No. 355.) A Caudle-Pot; inscribed with initials and date—

S
R · E
1687

Height 7 *in.; diameter* 11 *in.*
Coll. L.M.S.

1687. (No. 356.) An octagonal Plate; decorated in the centre with the Brewers' arms, and inscribed below with initials and date; the border being ornamented with a small conventional pattern of leaves and flowers.

Coll. L.M.S.

1687. (No. 357.) A Plate; inscribed in the centre, in a rather peculiar manner, with initials and date—

Diameter $8\frac{1}{2}$ *in.*
B. Mus. (*Franks Coll.*).

1687. (No. 358.) A Pair of Plates; inscribed with initials and date—

P
I · E
1687

Coll. H.G.

1688. (No. 359.) A Flower-Vase in the shape of a book; inscribed on both sides with legend, initials, and date—

The Gift Is Small
Good Will Is All

Length 5 *in.* COLL. DR. J.E.

1688. (No. 360.) A Plate; the rim moulded with ornamental pattern of shell-work in full relief. In the centre a representation of a man ploughing. Inscribed with initials and date, all in blue and yellow—

I ∴ C 1688

Diameter 9½ *in.*
COLL. LATE W.E.

1688. (No. 361.) Model of a Gabled House; decorated with figures, birds, foliage, and flowers, in blue and yellow, and inscribed with initials and date—

D · W
1688

COLL. LATE W.E.

1688. (No. 362.) A Plate; inscribed with initials and date—

P
W A
1688

Diameter 8½ *in.*
COLL. G.P.

1690. (No. 363.) A Dish; thin body, coated with greenish glaze, and painted in blue; subject, a Queen seated on a throne and receiving the presentation of a book. Inscribed—

Anno 1690

Diameter 15½ *in.* COLL. M.P.G.

1690. (No. 364.) A circular Plate; with inscription in a cartouche composed of a coronet, two winged dragons, and mask on the rim extending almost to centre—

Diameter 10 *in.* COLL. *J.H.*

1691. (No. 365.) A Pepper-Box, in the shape of a lantern; light green glaze, very roughly decorated in blue; pointed top; supported on four knobs. Inscribed with initials and date—

Height $8\frac{3}{4}$ *in.*; $3\frac{1}{2}$ *in. square.*
COLL. *H.W.*

1691. (No. 366.) A circular Plate; inscribed with initials and date on cartouche composed of dragons; mask, etc., on the upper portion.

Diameter 10 *in.*
B. MUS. (FRANKS COLL.).

1692. (No. 367.) A circular Plate; inscribed in a wreath with initials and date—

Diameter $8\frac{1}{2}$ *in.*
COLL. DR. *J.E.*

1693. (No. 368.) A circular Plate; decorated with cartouche towards one edge, and inscribed with initials and date—

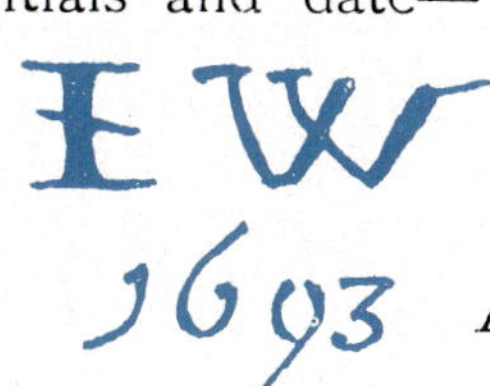

Diameter $8\frac{1}{2}$ *in.*
B. MUS. (FRANKS COLL.).

1693. (No. 369.) A circular Plate; inscribed with initials and date in a cartouche under a crown, with dragons as supporters. Similar to Nos. 364 and 366. Another resembling this in collection of late W. E.

MW
1693

Diameter $8\frac{1}{2}$ *in.*

COLL. *J.E.H.*

1693. (No. 370.) A Plate; decorated with panel enclosing initials and date—

H
B · C
1693

Diameter $8\frac{1}{2}$ *in.*

COLL. *B. MUS.*

1693. (No. 371.) A Plate; decorated with initials and date—

T
R · I
1693

COLL. *H.G.*

1694. (No. 372.) A Plate; decorated with initials and date on cartouche, on edge, extending towards centre. Similar to Nos. 364, 366, 369.

I · S ·
1694

Diameter $9\frac{3}{4}$ *in.*

COLL. *J.S.S.*

1695. (No. 373.) A Caudle-Pot, with two handles and a spout; slightly decorated in blue, and inscribed with initials and date—

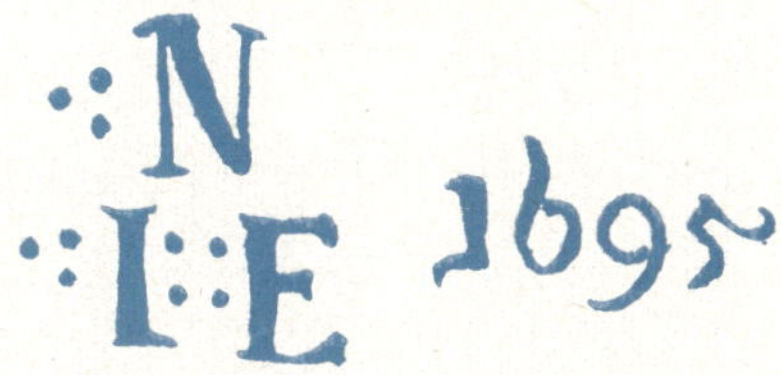

1697. (No. 374.) An oval Dish, in imitation of Palissy; coarse paste, coated with a brilliant greenish glaze, and painted in pale blue; the centre ornamented in low relief with a recumbent nude female figure, surrounded by five amorini; the border sunk in eight wells or godets, alternately circular and oval, painted with birds and flowers, and separated by baskets of flowers and marks in relief. Inscribed with initials and date. A similar specimen to No. 303 in B.M., dated 1659.

$19\frac{1}{2} \times 16\frac{1}{4}$.
Coll. M.P.G.

1697. (No. 375.) A Plate; decorated with half-length portraits of William and Mary in blue and yellow, and the initials W.M.R. Inscribed also with initials and date—

Diameter $8\frac{1}{2}$ *in.*
Coll. Dr. J.E.

1698. (No. 376.) A Plate; decorated with initials and date in cartouche on edge. Similar to Nos. 364, 368, 369.

G
A · E
1698

Diameter $10\frac{1}{4}$ *in.*
Coll. late W.E.

1698. (No. 377.) A Plate; inscribed with initials and date—

L
16 I E 98

1700. (No. 378.) A Drug-Pot, similar to No. 321 (dated 1666, Collection J.E.H.), but with Tudor Rose beneath the scroll. Bearing inscription and date—

S∴DE∴MECONIO
17 00

Height $7\frac{1}{2}$ *in.; diameter* $6\frac{3}{8}$ *in.* COLL. *J.E.H.*

1700. (No. 379.) A Drug-Pot; pair to the above.

S∴CAPIL∴VENER
17 00

Height $7\frac{1}{2}$ *in.; diameter* $6\frac{3}{8}$ *in.* COLL. *J.E.H.*

1700. (No. 380.) A Plate; inscribed with initials and date—

H
T·S
1700

COLL. *H.G.*

1704. (No. 381.) A Caudle-Cup; decorated in blue, and inscribed with initials and date—

Height $5\frac{3}{4}$ *in.; diameter* $6\frac{1}{2}$ *in.*
COLL. *T. MUS.*

17 C
04 I L MC

1705. (No. 382.) A Pot, with two handles; decorated with birds, flowers, and scrolls, and inscribed with initials and date—

Height 4¾ *in.; diameter* 6¼ *in.*
COLL. LATE *R.F.*

1707. (No. 383.) A circular Plate; decorated with cartouche towards one edge, and inscribed with initials and date—

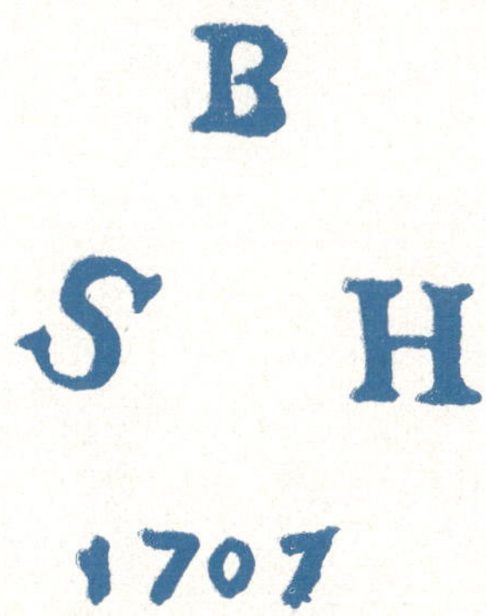

Diameter 9 *in.*
COLL. DR. *J.E.*

1710. (No. 384.) A circular Plate; inscribed in blue within wreath of same colour—

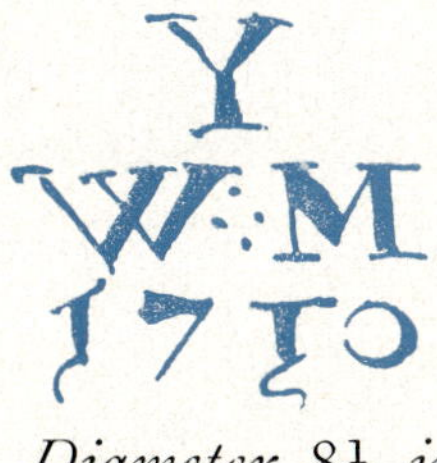

Diameter 8½ *in.*
COLL. *J.E.H.*

1713 (No. 385.) A Vessel in the shape of a Cat, seated; decorated and inscribed in blue—

Cat
i am ms Olivet.

1714. (No. 386.) A Drug-Pot, with spout and handle. Inscription in ornamental panel; below, initials and date—

S:BALSAMIC
W·I
1714

Height 7 in.
B. Mus. (Franks Coll.).

1715. (No. 387.) A circular Plate; inscribed in blue within wreath of same colour—

God Save King George
1715

Diameter 9 in.
Coll. Dr. J.E.

1716. (No. 388.) A circular Plate; inscription in dark blue within small wreath of same colour—

E·H
1716

Diameter 8½ in. Coll. E.H.

1722. (No. 389.) A circular Plate; decorated in blue in Oriental style, and inscribed with initials and date—

·S·P·
1722

Diameter 8½ in.

1722. (No. 390.) A circular Plate; inscribed with initials and date—

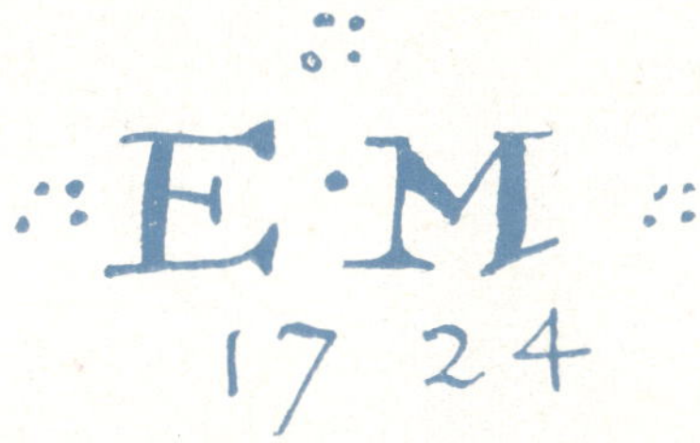

Diameter $8\frac{3}{4}$ *in.*
B. MUS. (FRANKS COLL.).

1728. (No. 391.) A Mug; prettily decorated with good conventional border at top, and sprays of flowers; a shoe (probably intended to indicate the trade of the persons for whom the mug was made) surmounts the cartouche containing some rough ornament but no arms—

Height 7 *in.; diameter* $5\frac{1}{2}$ *in.*
B. MUS. (FRANKS COLL.).

1729. (No. 392.) An oblong octagonal Tray; decorated in the centre with Flora, or Summer, in landscape. Inscribed on the back with initials and date in panel—

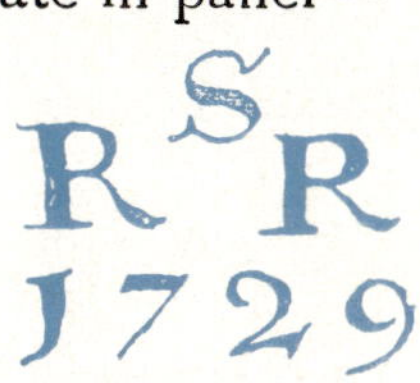

Length 17 *in.; Width* 13 *in.*
B. MUS. (FRANKS COLL.).

1731. (No. 393.) A circular Plate, inscribed with initials and date—

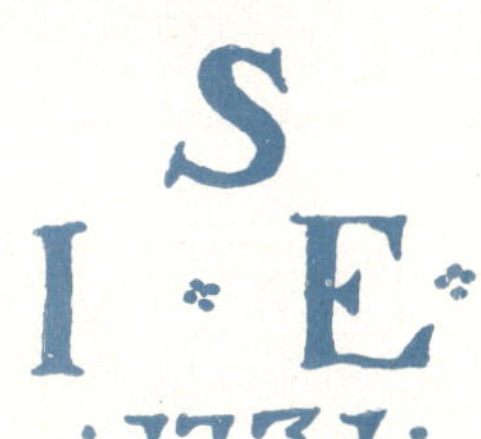

Diameter $8\frac{1}{8}$ *in.* COLL. DR. J.E.

1734. (No. 394.) A circular Plate; decorated in the centre with an inscription enclosed in wreath. (*See* No. 350, dated 1684, for a similar specimen.)

(2)
Let him Doo
what he Cann
1734

Diameter $8\frac{3}{4}$ *in.*
B. Mus. (*Franks Coll.*).

1736. (No. 395.) A circular Plate; similar to above.

(1)
What is a
merry Man
(1736)

Diameter $8\frac{1}{2}$ *in.*
B. Mus. (*Franks Coll.*).

1738. (No. 396.) A circular Plate; white glaze, decorated in brown; inscribed and dated—

To ye. Pious Memory
of Queen Caroline
*1738

Diameter 8 *in.*
Coll. T. Mus.

1742. (No. 397.) A circular Plate; similar to No. 375, dated 1736.

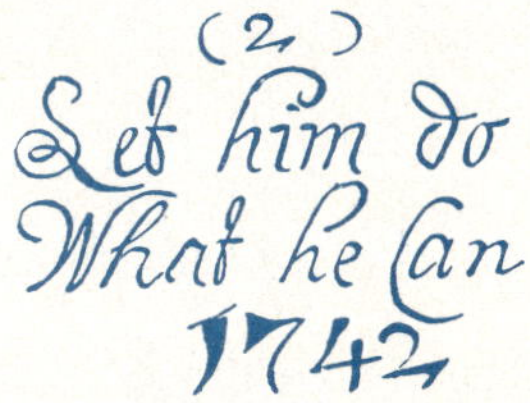

Diameter $8\frac{3}{4}$ *in.*
B. MUS. (FRANKS COLL.).

1742. (No. 398.) A circular Plate; similar to above, and belonging to same set.

Diameter $8\frac{3}{4}$ *in.*
B. MUS. (FRANKS COLL.).

1742. (No. 399.) A circular Plate; similar to above, and belonging to same set.

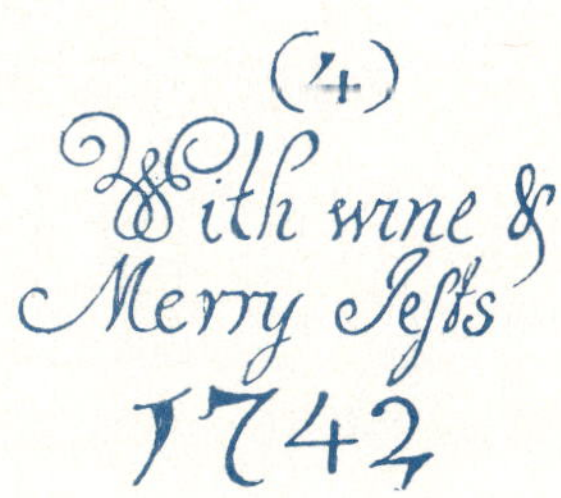

Diameter $8\frac{3}{4}$ *in.*
B. MUS. (FRANKS COLL.).

1742. (No. 400.) A circular Plate; similar to above, and belonging to same set.

Diameter $8\frac{3}{4}$ *in.*
B. MUS. (FRANKS COLL.).

1742. (No. 401.) A circular Plate; similar to above, and belonging to same set.

Diameter $8\frac{3}{4}$ *in.*

B. Mus. (*Franks Coll.*).

1746. (No. 402.) A very large circular Dish; decorated in blue with birds and floriated ornament. Inscription on back—

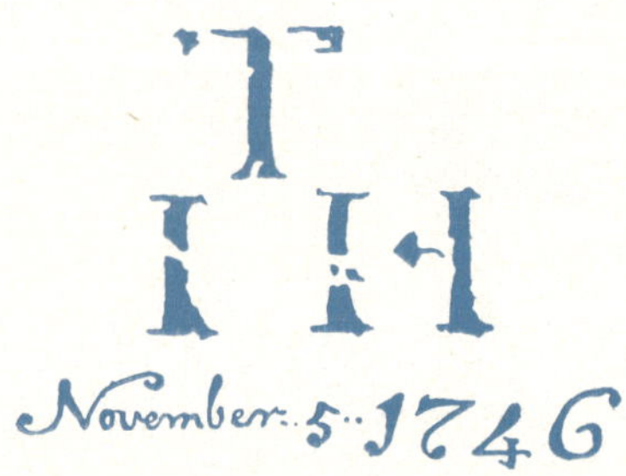

Diameter 2 *ft.*

Coll. J.H.

1797. (No. 403.) A Mug, mentioned by Mr. Jewitt as being in the possession of Mr. R. C. Ring; painted and signed by Doe, and said to be his last work, as he committed suicide on the 14th of September.

J. Doe, Sept. 1797.

(No. 404.) A circular Plate; pale green glaze of unusual shade. Decorated in the centre with two male figures in costume of the end of Charles II.'s reign, with swords, sashes, bands, epaulettes, wigs, and broad-brimmed hats; supporting on their hands, which touch, the nude figure of female twins joined by a ligament from the centre of their bodies. Surrounded by inscriptions. (*See* No. 207, dated 1680, for a piece commemorating the same event; also Note at end of volume, and frontispiece.)

BEHOVLD:TO:PARSONS:THAT:
ARE:RECONSILD:TO:ROB:
THE:PARENTS:AND:
TO:KEEP:THE:CHILD

HEARE:IS:GAIN:·O:THE:BROOM at their feet.

On the left of the twins AQILA, on the right PRISILA

Diameter $12\frac{5}{8}$ *in.* COLL. *J.E.H.*

(No 405.) A circular Plate; decorated in the centre with an inscription enclosed in wreath—

(1)

What is a Merry Man

Diameter 9 *in.* COLL. *J.E.H.*

(No. 406.) A circular Plate; similar to above, and belonging to same set.

(3)

To Entertain his Guest

Diameter 9 *in.* COLL. *J.E.H.*

(No. 407.) A circular Plate, similar to Nos. 405 and 406, and belonging to same set.

(4)

With Wine &
Merry Jest

Diameter 9 *in.* COLL. *J.E.H.*

(No. 408.) A circular Plate, similar to Nos. 405, 406, 407, and belonging to same set.

(5)

But if his Wife
does frown

Diameter 9 *in.* COLL. *J.E.H.*

(No. 409.) An octagonal Plate; decorated with an inscription in cartouche—

what is a
mery · man

Diameter 8 *in.* *B. Mus.* (FRANKS COLL.).

(No. 410.) An octagonal Plate, similar to above, and belonging to same set.

6
al · meryment
goos doune

Diameter 8 *in.* *B. Mus.* (FRANKS COLL.).

(No. 411.) A Wine-Jar, with a metal mount and lid; decorated in the front with a crown and inscription—

SACK
2
CR

Height $7\frac{1}{2}$ *in.; diameter* $5\frac{1}{2}$ *in.*
B. Mus. (*Franks Coll.*).

(No. 412.) A Wine-Jar; inscribed in front with name—

SACK

Coll. J.F.

(No. 413.) A large Wine-Jar; inscribed with name—

MARY BISH

Height $7\frac{1}{2}$ *in.; diameter* $4\frac{1}{2}$ *in.* *B. Mus.* (*Willett Coll.*).

(No. 414.) A Posset-Pot, with lid; decorated in blue, and with a rabbit painted inside.

DRINCK · YOVR · DRINK ·

Height $2\frac{1}{2}$ *in.; diameter* $3\frac{1}{2}$ *in.* *Coll. J.E.H.*

(No. 415.) A Puzzle-Jug; decorated with coat of arms, foliage, and initials in colours—

A M
D

Coll. late W.E.

(No. 416.) An Apothecary's Pill-Slab, in the shape of a shield; decorated with the arms, supporters, and motto of the Apothecaries' Company.

OPIFER QUE PER ORBEM DICOR

Length 10 *in.; width* 10½ *in.*

COLL. *J.E.H.*

A similar specimen in Mayer Museum, Liverpool.

Length 12 *in.; diameter* 10¼ *in.*

Also in *M. P. G.* and *S. K. Mus.*

(No. 417.) A Cup, with one handle; speckled purple ground, decorated with a white scroll with blue border, and inscription in blue—

:Drink:and:
wellcome:Sur:

Height 3 *in.; diameter* 3 *in.*

COLL. *B. Mus.*

(No. 418.) A Barber's Basin, broken; decorated inside, on the bottom, with various barber's implements; inscription on rim—

SIR: YOVRE :QVARTER:
IS:VP:

Diameter 10½ *in*
B. Mus.
(*Willett Coll.*);
also S. K. Coll.

(No. 419.) A Jug; inscribed in front in blue—

J. Fawsit
37 = *Paddington St*
Mary Le Bone

Height 5 *in.;*
diameter 3 *in.*
COLL. *N.C. Mus.*

(No. 420.) A Pap-Boat; decorated with flowers and spots in blue, and inscribed in maroon—

Boy

Length 4½ *in.* *B. Mus.* (*Willett Coll.*).

(No. 421.) A circular Dish; decorated in blue, yellow, green, and maroon. In the centre the Temptation is represented, with the figures of Adam and Eve, the Serpent and various animals adorning the landscape. A fine border, of fruit, is well designed, and recalls the style of the decorations on Italian majolica. Inscribed over the heads of the figures with their names—

ADAM EVE

Diameter 16¾ *in.* *B. Mus.* (*Willett Coll.*).

(No. 422.) A circular Plate; inscribed within wreath—

Duke William For Ever

Diameter 7¾ *in.* *B. Mus.* (*Franks Coll.*).

(No. 423.) An oval Dish, very similar to No. 303, dated 1659; this specimen, however, though decorated in the centre with the same subject, and a border formed of alternate circles and ovals, is not inscribed with initials and date, the arms of the City of London, and the arms of the Pewterers' Company on the rim, as is the specimen in the British Museum, but is decorated in centre of the dish with the arms of the City of London between those of the Dyers' and Cutlers' Companies, and inscribed below with name—

EDWARD· HALL : M·A·R

On the back  19½ *in.* × 16 *in.*

Coll. Mrs. W.P.

(No. 424.) A very large Drug-Pot, of the usual style; made to hold a balsam prepared by Dr. Thoroton, author of "The History of Nottinghamshire," printed in folio, 1677. He died November, 1678. It is possible that the jar was made for the doctor himself. Inscription in blue on a white band—

BALS: D^{R}: THORE^{TON}

Height 12 *in.*

(No. 425.) A Puzzle-Jug, with handle and three spouts; perforated at upper part; bluish-white glaze, with inscription and flowing ornament in pale blue.

Here Gentlemen Come try your Skill . .
I'll hold a Wager if you will . . . .
That you Don't Drink this liq^{r} all
Without you Spill or lett some Fall .

COLL. L. MUS.

(No. 426.) An octagonal Plate, with inscription in arabesque frame. (*See* Nos. 409, 410, to which set this may probably belong.)

A
whit wyne
and mery gels

$7\frac{1}{2}$ *in.* × $8\frac{1}{4}$ *in.*
COLL. DR. J.E.

BRISTOL DELFT.

THE most marked distinctions between this ware and the preceding are the following: the glaze is thinner and harder, and, as a rule, possesses, instead of the pure white of the Lambeth specimens, a slight but distinct greenish-blue tint. The decoration is usually in a deeper and more positive blue, and is to a large extent based upon Oriental, though not unfrequently upon Dutch, designs. A not uncommon accompaniment to this treatment in blue is a decoration of floral character in pure white "*bianca sopra bianca*," which may, we think, be considered to afford a pretty positive identification of the origin of any specimen of English Delft upon which it occurs. The names of the two most celebrated potters of Bristol Delft were Richard Frank and Joseph Flower, and pieces well known to have been made by each are in existence. The plates decorated by Michael Edkins were certainly the production of Frank's factory, and it seems to us that the glaze of these does not possess in so marked a degree the peculiar greenish hue above alluded to, and usually found in pieces of Bristol Delft; whilst their imitation of Nankin Porcelain is, as has been observed in the Preface, so close as to be almost deceptive at a short distance. Besides plates, punch-bowls in considerable numbers, mugs, jugs, tankards, tea-poys, sponge-dishes, and some smaller pieces, have been preserved. The colours employed in the decoration of this ware are more numerous and more freely employed than those to be found in Lambeth Delft; and red, puce, brown, and yellow are to be found in conjunction. It is with considerable diffidence that we ascribe the first five pieces in our list (dates from 1676 to 1705) to Bristol, and we feel that we may still have to bow to Professor Church's dictum—that the earliest date may really be 1706.

1676. (No. 427.) A Wine-Jar; highly glazed, and decorated in blue on the white tin enamel. We have not seen this piece, and are therefore unable to assign, with any confidence, so puzzling a specimen to an undoubted origin. The shape is unusual for Bristol Delft, and the date earlier than that which we are accustomed to connect with this ware; but the lettering bears decidedly English characteristics, and the decoration can hardly be attributed to Lambeth. We leave it here *ad referendum* with all reserve.

Height 7 in. Diameter $3\frac{3}{4}$ in. *Coll. A.E.C.*

1680. (No. 428.) A circular Plate; glaze bluish-white, decorated in blue in the Chinese style. Inscribed with initials and date. This piece, and the nine which immediately follow it, are *provisionally* ascribed to Bristol, for reasons analogous to those given above.

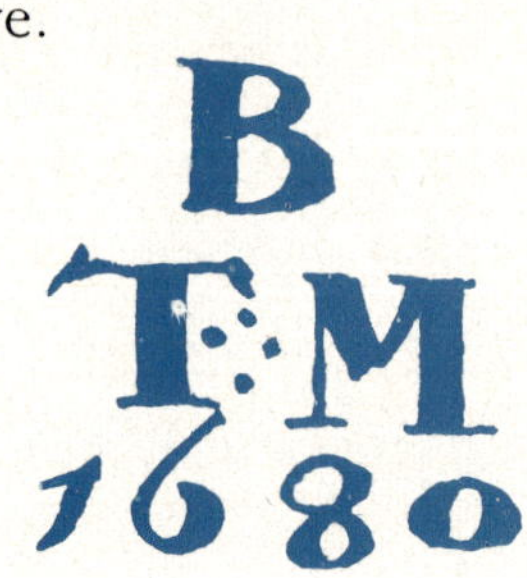

Diameter $8\frac{5}{8}$ in. *Coll. J.E.H.*

(16)92. (No. 429.) A Pair of Shoes, with high heels and large bows; white glaze, blue line decoration. Inscribed with initials and date—

AH
92

Height $3\frac{1}{2}$ *in.; length* 6 *in.* COLL. *J.E.H.*

1703. (No. 430.) A Plate, marked on the rim with initials and date; of a very nice quality, with a good glaze, and the blue of a good colour. Mentioned by Mr. Jewitt.

B
S M
1703

1705. (No. 431.) Two high-heeled Shoes; mentioned by Mr. Jewitt. Inscribed with initials and date—

MI 1705

1706. (No. 432.) A Bowl, decorated in blue with conventional flowers, etc. Inscribed with initials and date—

C
C I
1706

Height 8 *in.;*
diameter $15\frac{1}{2}$ *in.*

COLL. *MRS. T.*

1706. (No. 433.) A round Dish, ornamented in blue; mentioned by Professor Church. Inscribed with initials and date—

P
B∴M
1706

1707. (No 434.) A High-heeled Shoe; white glaze, decorated in blue with conventional flowers and birds in the Japanese style. Inscribed with initials and date—

17ER07

Height 4¾ *in.; length* 2¼ *in.*

Coll. D. Mus.

1707. (No. 435.) A Two-handled Posset-Pot, of rather florid design. White glaze, decorated in blue with borders of conventional character, and with roughly executed drawings of figures and landscape on each side. Initials and date inside Pot—

E∴W
1707

Height 4¾ *in.; Diameter* 5 *in.* *Coll. J.E.H.*

1710. (No. 436.) A Flower-holder in the form of a clasped book. White glaze covered with rather coarse blue decoration. The clasps of yellowish colour. Inscribed with initials and date—

J7 I HJO

Width $3\frac{3}{4}$ *in.; length* $5\frac{3}{4}$ *in.*
COLL. *J.E.H.*

1711. (No. 437.) A Plate; decorated in blue with landscape. Inscribed with initials and date—

P
W·M
1711

Diameter $8\frac{3}{4}$ *in.*
COLL. *A.W.F.*

1716. (No. 438.) A pair of Plates, ornamented in blue; presented to the possessor by a descendant of the family of Davis, for whom they were made. Considered to be the earliest pieces of Bristol with authenticated history, but maker's name unknown. Inscribed with initials and date—

D
T × H
1716

COLL. LATE *W.E.*

1716. (No. 439.) A circular Plate, with inscription and date—

God save King George . 1716.

COLL. *L. MUS.*
A similar specimen in COLL. *H.W.*

1721. (No. 440.) A circular Plate; decorated with landscape, and inscribed with initials and date—

Diameter $8\frac{3}{4}$ *in.*
B. Mus. (*Franks Coll.*).

1722. (No. 441.) A Tea-Poy; mentioned by Professor Church. Inscribed with initials and date—

K.F.W. 1722

1722. (No. 442.) A high-heeled Shoe or Choppine; mentioned by Mr. Jewitt. Inscribed on the sole with initials and date—

MS
1722

1731. (No. 443.) A Punch-Bowl; painted in blue with scrolls on the outside, and inscribed on the inside with verses and date—

John Udy of Luxillion
his tin was ſo fine
it gliderd this punch bowl
and made it to shine
pray fill it with punch
lett the tinners ſill round
they never will budge
till the bottom they ſound

1731

Diameter $10\frac{1}{4}$ *in.* *Coll. M.P.G.*

1734. (No. 444.) A circular Plate; decorated in rich blue with a full-length portrait of a man (probably a local celebrity) seated on a chair. The subject covers the entire centre of the plate; the rim decorated with a rich pattern of scroll-work. Inscribed on the back with initials and date. An early and interesting specimen.

TG
1734

Diameter $8\frac{5}{8}$ *in.*

COLL. LATE W.E.

1735. (No. 445.) An octagonal Plate; decorated with Chinese subjects, and inscribed with name and date—

IOANNA+IAMES
1735

Diameter $8\frac{1}{2}$ *in.*

COLL. DR. M.

1735. (No. 446.) A circular Plate; inscribed on the back with initials and date, and on the margin with smaller letters—

R:S
October ye 27th
1735

·S S·
1735

COLL. B. MUS.

1738. (No. 447.) A circular Plate; inscribed with name and date. Mentioned by Professor Church.

Elizabeth
Barness
1738.

1740. (No. 448.) A circular Plate; inscribed on rim with initials and date. Mentioned by Mr. Jewitt.

P
17 40
R.S

1739. (No. 449.) A circular Plate; bluish-white glaze, decorated in blue. Circle in centre, quaint floral ornament within and without. Inscribed on the back with initials and date—

W B
1739

Diameter $8\frac{5}{8}$ *in.*
COLL. *J.E.H.*

1739. (No. 450.) A circular Plate; a similar specimen and fellow to above.

I.B
1739

Diameter $8\frac{5}{8}$ *in.*
COLL. *J.E.H.*

1741–2. (No. 451.) A Plate; painted with a view of the river Avon and the old Hotwells House. Inscribed with date. Mentioned by Mr. Jewitt as being in the possession of Mr. J. Flower Fussell.

1742. (No. 452.) A circular Plate; decorated in Chinese style. Inscribed with initials and date on rim. Orange edge.

A E
1742

Diameter $8\frac{1}{4}$ *in.*
COLL. *J.H.*

1744. (No. 453.) A Mug or Tankard; decorated with Chinese pattern, and inscribed with name and date—

Margret Latham 1744

Height 6 *in.; diameter* 4 *in.* *B.* MUS. (WILLETT COLL.).

1744. (No. 454.) A Plate; inscribed with initials and date. Mentioned by Professor Church.

B

S ∴ E

1744

1747. (No. 455.) An oval Dish, with perforated edge; decorated with figure of St. George and the Dragon, and inscribed with initials and date—

B ∴ S

1747

COLL. L. MUS.

1748. (No. 456.) A circular Plate, painted in blue in Oriental style; in the centre a garden scene, with a lady and two attendants, one of whom is holding a large umbrella over her. Inscribed in the centre with initials and date. Beyond are two borders of flowers and diaper patterns.

T

I F

1748

Diameter 9 *in.*

S. K. MUS. (SCHREIBER COLL.).

1749. (No. 457.) A Bowl; decorated in blue with a well-drawn figure of the Young Pretender in tartan coat, laced breeches, and stockings; small cap on head; sword in right hand, with the left he points to a crown. On the ground a target and pistols, above all some bold ornament, under which the motto—

AUDENTIOR : IBO

ALL OR NONE :

I S

1749

Inscribed with initials and date. *Height* $4\frac{1}{4}$ *in.; diameter* 10 *in.* COLL. B. MUS.

1749. (No. 458.) A Punch-Bowl; painted in blue, red, yellow, and green; decorated with flowers on the inside, and armorial bearings with motto on the outside—*God grant unity.* Inscribed on the bottom in blue with initials and date—

Diameter 12 *in.*

COLL. *M.P.G.*

1750. (No. 459.) A Plate, belonging to a dinner-service made by Joseph Flower (mentioned by Mr. Jewitt as being in the possession of a descendant—Mr. O. Flower Fussell). The different pieces bear initials and dates varying from 1742 to 1750.

1751. (No. 460.) A Plate; mentioned by Professor Church. Inscribed with initials and date—

H
S x H
1751

1752. (No. 461.) A Christening-Bowl; mentioned by Professor Church. Inscribed with name and date—

Hannah Hopkins, born September 17 *new style,* 1752.

1752. (No. 462.) A Tile, mentioned by Professor Church, representing a dog. Inscribed with the word Bristol and the date 1752.

1754. (No. 463.) An Election-Plate; mentioned by Professor Church. Inscribed with name and date—

NUGENT ONLY
1754

1754. (No. 464.) An Election-Plate; mentioned by Professor Church.

Calvert and Martin
for Tukesbury
1754

1754. (No. 465.) An Election-Plate; similar to above. Inscribed with name and date; the ground sprinkled with maroon.

Calvert and Martin
For Ever
1754
Sold by Webb

Diameter 13¼ *in.* *B. Mus.* (*Franks Coll.*); *also Coll. L. Mus.*

1754. (No. 466.) An Election-Plate; the ground is powdered; bouquets in small panels on the rim; in the centre a medallion with inscription and date—

SIR I^{no} Pole For Ever
1754.

Diameter 8⅞ *in.* *Coll. B. Mus., late W.E.*

1754. (No. 467.) A circular Plate; decorated in the centre with a vessel at sea, beneath which is inscription; a narrow border of diaper pattern.

THE UNION. HA KLINCKERT·

N. 1754

Diameter $8\frac{3}{4}$ *in.*
SCHREIBER COLL.

1754. (No. 468.) A deep circular Plate, decorated in Chinese style. Inscribed on the back with name and date—

Iohn Saunders
1754

Diameter $8\frac{1}{2}$ *in.* COLL. *J.E.H.*;
also COLL. *B. Mus.*, LATE *W.E.*

1755. (No. 469.) A Bowl; highly decorated on the outside with floral pattern in blue, and inside (*pâte sur pâte*) with white flowers, and inscribed with motto and date—

One · bowl · more
and · then
1755

Diameter $13\frac{3}{4}$ *in.* COLL. *J.E.H.*

1755. (No. 470.) A fine Bowl; inscribed on the foot with initials and date—

W·:·C
1755

1757. (No. 471.) A large Bowl; very prettily decorated in colours with flowers, and one female figure. Inscribed with motto and date—

Now friends are mett
Lets drink and Sing
A health to George
Our Brittish king
*Decb: th*1. 1757

Height $5\frac{1}{2}$ *in.*; *diameter* $10\frac{1}{2}$ *in.*
COLL. *H.W.*

1758. (No. 472.) A Tankard and Cover, coated with a greenish glaze; painted in blue with landscape, and dated at base of handle. The cover ornamented with portrait of Queen Anne. Inscription inside, probably Bristol.

L.C. Pope
1758

Height 11 *in.*
COLL. *M.P.G.*

1760. (No. 473.) A circular Plate; made at the Delft Ware Manufactory of Richard Frank, Redcliff Back, Bristol. Painted by Michael Edkins (grandfather of the late owner). Decorated with a landscape with figures, cattle, and birds, in blue, in the Chinese style. Inscribed on the back with the initials of the painter and his wife—

E
M·B
1760

Diameter $8\frac{3}{4}$ *in.*
COLL. LATE *W.E.*; *also* COLL. *M.P.G.*

1760. (No. 474.) A Tea-Poy, mentioned by Professor Church; inscribed with initials and date—

U. D. 1760

1760. (No. 475.) **Bristol** (?). A Plate, with scalloped edge. Decorated with Chinese landscape in colours, and inscribed on back with name and date—

Cornelius Dixon
Norwich
1760

Diameter 9 *in.*
B. MUS. (WILLETT COLL.).

1761. (No. 476.) A fine circular Dish, with a waved margin; dated and signed by the decorator. It is a good example of British Delft. The landscape is clear blue, with figures in the peculiar manganese colour that is characteristic of the Bristol pottery. Mentioned by Messrs. Owen and Jewitt.

ye 1st Septr
1761
Bowen fecit

1763. (No. 477.) A circular Plate; greyish, border in white work; decorated in blue with man on horseback; inscription and date on edge—

A·BOSAVERN·LOOE
1763 *Diameter* 9 *in* *Coll. — D.*

Another Plate, of same date, mentioned by Professor Church.

1763. (No. 478.) A Plate; mentioned by Professor Church. Inscribed with initials and date—

P
J B
1763

1765. (No. 479.) A Tankard; decorated with landscape and ruins; on lid copy of Queen Anne crown; date on lower part of handle—

JJ
65

Height $8\frac{1}{4}$ *in.*
B. Mus. (*Franks Coll.*)

1767. (No. 480.) A Plate, mentioned by Professor Church. Inscribed with initials and date—

E
F · G
1767

1768. (No. 481.) A Jug, in white glazed earthenware; lobed body, blue edge, and painted with flowers by Fifield when in the 75th year of his age; inscription in front—

Mary King, born August 21st 1768

and stamped on the base— POUNTNEY & ALLIES.

1771. (No. 482.) A Pair of Soup-Plates; decorated in Chinese style, blue on a white ground, orange rim.

E
B * E
E
1771.

Diameter 9 *in.* COLL. *J.H.*

1773. (No. 483.) A Punch-Bowl; decorated with fine floral ornament in blue on the outside, and inscribed on the inside—

One Bowl
More & then
H
T ⁝ M
1773.

Height 4 *in.*; *diameter* 10¼ *in.* COLL. *J.E.H.*

1784. (No. 484.) A Bottle, flat-sided, with ring-shaped body; coated with greenish glaze. Printed in blue with flowers on one side and landscape on the other, and inscribed around the hoop of the body—

James and Ann Tompson

1784

COLL. *M.P.G.*

BRISTOL DELFT, UNDATED.

(No. 485.) A large Bowl; ornamented on the outside with Chinese subject in blue and brown-pink; inside *bianca sopra bianca* ornamentation, in the centre inscription in blue—

Succefs
To the Britifh
Arms

Height 4½ *in.; diameter* 10½ *in.* COLL. *J.E.H.*

(No. 486.) A Bowl; an exactly similar specimen to above, but a little smaller.

Height 3¼ *in.; diameter* 7½ *in.* COLL. *J.H.*

Similar specimens also in B. Mus. (Franks Coll.) and Coll. Mr. Doel.

(No. 487.) A Puzzle-Jug, with a handle and three spouts, perforated at upper part; bluish-white glaze, with inscription and flowing ornament in pale blue—

Here Gentlemen com Try your Skill
I'll hold a wager if you will
That you don't Drink this Liqur all
With-out you Spill or Let Some Fall.

Height 7 in.; diameter 5½ in. COLL. *J.E.H.*

(No. 488.) A Puzzle-Jug; very similar in character to above.

Here Gentlemen come try your Skill
I'll hould a Wager if you will . . . .
That you dont Drink this Liquor all . . .
Without you spill or let some fall . . . .

Height 7 in.; diameter 5¼ in. COLL. *J.E.H.*

(No. 489.) A Puzzle-Jug; very similar in character and inscription to above specimens. Bears in addition the initials—

P M

Height 6½ in.; diameter 5¼ in. COLL. *M.B.*

(No. 490.) A Plate, with scalloped edges; hand-painted in pale blue with arms of the guild of Basket Makers. A very interesting illustration of these arms is to be found in an engraving (of much later date than the plate) given to the possessor by the late Mr. Edkins of Bristol. The same arms are shown as on the plate, but with the addition of two griffins as supporters. A pollard willow and a bundle of twigs flank the whole. Above the device are the words "The Basket Makers' Arms," and below is the inscription "Jas. Weeks B. M. (Basket Maker) Bristol 1804. Dodrell sculp."

LET US LOUE ONE ANOTHER

Diameter 7⅞ in. COLL. *J.E.H., also J.H.*

(No. 491.) A Bowl; decorated with landscape, and inscribed on the inside—

Success to
Trade

A similar specimen, but smaller. *Height* $4\frac{1}{4}$ *in.; diameter* $10\frac{1}{4}$ *in.*
COLL. *M.P.G.* B. MUS. (WILLETT COLL.).

(No. 492.) A Bowl; decorated on the inside with a view of a tinworks, and bearing inscription—

Success to Iohn Blewett Esqr
& Co

Diameter 14 *in.*
COLL. MAYER MUS.

(No. 493.) A circular Plate; decorated in the centre with a half-length portrait of the King of Prussia, and inscribed with initials—

K P

Diameter $8\frac{3}{4}$ *in.*
COLL. LATE *W.E.*

(No. 494.) A Bowl; inscribed on the inside—

One more and then

Height $3\frac{1}{4}$ *in.; diameter* $7\frac{3}{4}$ *in.* B MUS. (FRANKS COLL.).

(No. 495.) A circular Plate; decorated in the centre with head of a man with horns, and inscribed with initials—

F.P.

COLL. L. MUS.

(No. 496.) A square Plaque; painted in blue; two girls with birds; in the background a landscape with ruins. Inscribed at the back in blue—

E } TAYLOR
A }

Diameter $11\frac{1}{2}$ *in.* × $11\frac{1}{2}$ *in.* *S. K. Mus.* (*Schreiber Coll.*).

(No. 497.) A large Platter; white, with orange edge; on rim coat of arms, in blue (? Farmer family); inscribed on back with double cipher in blue—

Depth $2\frac{1}{4}$ *in.; diameter* $17\frac{7}{8}$ *in.*
Coll. J.H.

(No. 498.) A Dish; decorated in Chinese style, and inscribed with names—

Jacob and Rebecca Anobas.

Diameter $11\frac{1}{2}$ *in.* *B. Mus.* (*Willett Coll.*).

(No. 499.) A Dish; decorated in a similar style to above, and inscribed with names—

Benj^{a} & Deborah Nones

Diameter $11\frac{1}{4}$ *in.* *B. Mus.* (*Willett Coll.*).

(No. 500.) A Dish; decorated in Chinese style, and inscribed with names—

Abraham & Sarah
Brandon

Diameter $12\frac{3}{4}$ *in.* *B. Mus.* (*Willett Coll.*).

(No. 501.) A Dish; decorated with figure of the Duke of Cumberland on horseback. Inscription on edge—

God ſaue y^{e} Duke of Comberland
Remember y^{e} fight of Culloden.

Diameter 13 *in.* *B. Mus.* (*Willett Coll.*).

(No. 502.) An octagonal Plate; decorated in centre with tea-drinking scene. Inscribed on the back with initials—

E
WQ

Diameter $8\frac{1}{2}$ *in.*
B. Mus. (*Willett Coll.*).

(No. 503.) An Election-Plate, decorated with woolsack; ground sprinkled with maroon.

Calvert & Martin
For Tukesbury
Sold by Webb

Diameter 9 *in.* *B. Mus.* (*Franks Coll.*).

Two similar specimens in Mayer Museum, Liverpool.

(No. 504.) An Election-Plate; inscribed with names referring to an election which took place in Taunton in 1768.

Coll. T. Mus.

LIVERPOOL DELFT.

IT is very difficult to draw up a list of the characteristics which distinguish Liverpool from Bristol Delft. The glaze of the former is usually of a bluish tint, and apt to be filled with small holes, owing to the absorbent character of the body. One important variety, however, may be readily distinguished after some practice, as it differs not only from other Liverpool Delft, but from all other English Faïence: we allude to that made by Thomas Fazackerley. This possesses a fine white glaze, hard and opaque, and is usually decorated with a variety of colours, dark-blue, sage-green, orange-red, pale lemon-yellow, etc., which have generally been so fully absorbed into the glaze as to leave the place of application unglazed and dead. The blue pigment frequently runs into the glaze, as if it had been applied whilst very wet. The forms of this ware are mainly confined to plates, dishes, mugs, and char-pots. The ordinary Liverpool Delft is constantly to be found in the shape of bowls, which not unfrequently bear inscriptions connected with maritime commerce, and many of these doubtless exist in addition to those which have come under our notice.

The dates of our specimens range from 1702 downwards.

1702. (No. 505.) A Caudle-Pot, with lid and two handles, one of which is broken; beautifully decorated in blue with pastoral scenes, and inscribed under the lip with initials and date. A very fine and interesting specimen.

S
I B
17 02

Height 11½ *in.*

COLL. L. MUS.

1716. (No. 506.) A large, flat, oblong Plaque; composed of the ordinary buff-coloured clay, covered with tin enamel, on which the design is drawn in blue, and then glazed. The plaque represents the village of Great Crosby, as seen from the Mersey, and bears the name and date on a ribbon at the top—

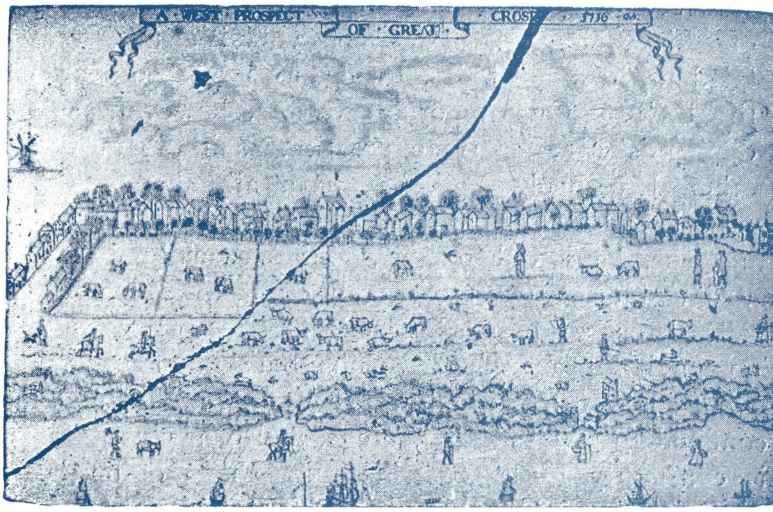

A · WEST · PROSPECT · OF · GREAT · CROSBY · 1716 ·

2 ft. 7 in. × 1 ft. 8 in. *Coll. L. Mus.*

1722. (No. 507.) A curious Plaque, affixed to the wall over one of the seats of Old Crosby Church, bearing the arms of the Merchant Taylors' Company and an inscription. John and Henry Harrison are said to have been natives of Crosby, the Grammar School of which village they erected and endowed, after having made large fortunes as merchants in London, the trust being held by the Company of Merchant Taylors. Mentioned and illustrated by Mr. Jewitt.

THIS ∵ SEAT ∵ WAS ERECTED BY
JOHN ∵ HARRISON ∵ AND
HENRY ∵ HARRISON : OF
LEVERPOOLE 1722

1728. (No. 508.) A Mug; decorated in blue, and inscribed in front with initials and date—

Height 6 in.
Coll. L. Mus.

1733. (No. 509.) A Puzzle-Jug, with handle and three spouts, perforated at upper part; white glaze, decorated with dark-blue, rather crude, ornament. Inscribed with motto and date—

Here Gentlemen com try your skill
I'll hold a wager if you will
That you don't drink this liquor all
Without you spill or lett some fall.

1733

Height $7\frac{1}{2}$ *in.; diameter* $5\frac{3}{4}$ *in.*

COLL. *J.E.H.*

This is a puzzling specimen, and ought perhaps to be inserted under the heading of Uncertain Delft. However, it appears to more closely resemble Liverpool than either Lambeth or Bristol.

1736. (No. 510.) A Punch-Bowl; ornamented in blue with flowers, and inscribed with motto and date—

PARLIMENT BOWL FREE WITHOUT EXCISE.

1736

alluding to the taking off the duty by Walpole's Bill.

Diameter 14 *in.* COLL. *M.P.G.*

1753. (No. 511.) A very large, circular Plaque, in front of a house at Newton-cum-Larton, in the parish of West Kirby, in Cheshire; decorated with the arms of Johnson impaling those of Auton, and inscribed beneath with date. The Mr. Johnson here alluded to was Mayor of Liverpool in 1766. Having married an heiress, Miss Auton, he built the house above mentioned, and here resided for several years; the slab, which was probably the gift of his brother Alderman, Mr. Shaw the potter, having been placed in front of the building. Mentioned by Mr. Mayer in his "History of the Art of Pottery in Liverpool."

1757. (No. 512.) A Mug; decorated with flowers in yellow, green, blue, and purple. Inscribed in blue with initials and date. Said by Mr. Jewitt to have been made for Thomas Fazackerley by a workman in Samuel Shaw's employ; but Mr. Mayer, in his pamphlet "History of the Art of Pottery in Liverpool," says that they were made by Thomas Fazackerley, who was himself a workman in the Shaw Potteries.

T. F. 1757 *Height* $6\frac{1}{4}$ *in.* *Coll. L. Mus.*

1758. (No. 513.) A Mug, similar to above, but smaller; decorated in the same style, and evidently produced by the same hand. Inscribed on the front, within an oval, with initials and date, the former being evidently intended for Catherine Fazackerley, wife of the Thomas Fazackerley mentioned above.

C F
1758

Height $4\frac{7}{8}$ *in.*
Coll. L. Mus.

1760. (No. 514.) A Bowl; decorated on the outside with birds, butterflies, and flowers, and on the inside with a ship in full sail, and below an inscription and date—

Succeſs to the Monmouth
1760

Height 4 *in.; diameter* $10\frac{1}{2}$ *in.* *Coll. L. Mus.*

1766. (No. 515.) A Punch-Bowl; decorated on the inside with a ship in full sail, and below an inscription and date—

Succeſs to the Friend-ship
1766

Diameter $9\frac{1}{2}$ *in.* *Coll. M.P.G.*

1769. (No. 516.) A Bowl; decorated on the outside with floral ornamentation. Inside, in the centre, the figure of a man, bareheaded, with axe in his hands, looking towards the left, on which side are inscription and date—

B
A ÷ E
1769

Height $3\frac{1}{8}$ *in.; diameter* $7\frac{1}{4}$ *in.*
COLL. *J.H.*

1772. (No. 517.) A Tea-Pot, of the ordinary yellow glaze, with flowers roughly painted on one side, with black lines for leaves. Inscribed on the other side with names and date—

Iohn & Mary
Wheeldon 1772

Height $5\frac{1}{2}$ *in.; diameter* 7 *in.* COLL. *A.E.C.*

1775. (No. 518.) A Jug; decorated on one side with initials and date, on the other with the figure of a man in the costume of the period, in plum-coloured coat, pink flapped vest, yellow breeches, and a black skull-cap, standing in a garden with a spade and a beer-glass in his hands. The lip represents a woman's face, with black hair and tiara.

B
T C
1775

Height 9 *in.; diameter* $5\frac{1}{2}$ *in.*
COLL. *DR. H.N.*

1779. (No. 519.) A Punch-Bowl; decorated on the outside with the figures of two sailors, the one sitting on the stock of an anchor, and the other astride of a barrel; between them a large chest, on which is written "Spanish Gold." On the inside a ship in full sail, and below inscription and date. The whole decoration in blue.

1779 : Success to the Isabella. COLL. *L. MUS.*

LIVERPOOL DELFT, UNDATED.

(No. 520.) A Punch-Bowl; decorated in blue, on the outside with fine floral ornament, on the inside with inscription—

Trade and Navigation

Diameter 10¾ *in.* Coll. *J.E.H.*

(No. 521.) A Punch-Bowl; decorated with flowers in green, blue, purple, and yellow, in panels, on mottled purple ground; bottom of the bowl inscribed inside, in blue—

One Bowle more & then

Coll. *M.P.G.; also* Coll. *T.B.*

(No. 522.) A very large Punch-Bowl; said to have been made by Pennington, and painted by John Robinson, a workman in Pennington's employ. It is decorated on the outside with landscape and figures, and on the inside with ships in full sail, with inscription below, and surrounded by a deep border of trophies of warlike implements arranged in six groups, which are divided by different kinds of shot. Robinson subsequently removed into Staffordshire, and ultimately presented the bowl to the Potteries Mechanics' Institution, where it is still carefully preserved along with his note—"John Robinson, a pot-painter, served his time at Pennington's, in Shaw's Brow, and there painted this punch-bowl." Inscribed—

Succeſs to the Africa Trade
George Dickinſon

Height 9 *in.; diameter* 20½ *in.* Coll. *P.M.I.*

(No 523.) A Punch-Bowl; decorated in blue, and inscribed with motto—

Fill up the bowl — *Height* 3½ *in.; diameter* 9 *in.* Coll. *A.E.C.*

(No. 524.) A Punch-Bowl; similar to above, and inscribed with motto—

Success to the British Arms. — *Height* 5 *in.; diameter* 11 *in.* Coll. *A.E.C.*

(No. 525.) A Plate, with scalloped edge; decorated in centre in Chinese style. Inscribed on the back—

Miſs Betty Brownwell

Diameter 7½ *in.* Coll. *J.H.*

(No. 526.) A Punch-Bowl; decorated on the outside with flowers in Chinese style, on the inside with ship in full sail. Inscribed—

Succefs to the Active
Ioseph and Elizabeth.

Diameter $10\frac{3}{4}$ *in.*

(No. 527.) A Punch-Bowl; decorated on the outside with a ship in full sail, and inscribed on the inside—

Succefs to the Blundell *Coll. L. Mus.*

(No. 528.) A Punch-Bowl; decorated on the outside with conventional flowers, and inscribed on the inside—

THE NANCY *Coll. L. Mus.*

(No. 529.) A Punch-Bowl; decorated with ship in blue, and a border inside and out in green, yellow, and brown. Inscribed on the inside—

Success to the William & Mary

Coll. L. Mus.

(No. 530.) Two Puzzle-Jugs, of the usual style and decoration. Inscribed—

Here Gentlemen, come try y^{r} skill, &c.

Coll. L. Mus.

(No. 531.) A Mug; decorated in blue with coat of arms, and inscribed—

GOD GRANT UNITY

Height $6\frac{1}{4}$ *in.; diameter* 4 *in.* *Coll. H.W.*

(No. 532.) A Flower-Vase; elaborately painted in blue, and inscribed with initials on the bottom—

D W A *Coll. L. Mus.*

(No. 533.) A round, open Pot, for preserved fish, with figures of fish painted round it. Inscribed with initials—

I B *Coll. L. Mus.*

STAFFORDSHIRE DELFT.

THIS ware, although often from its very crudity remarkably picturesque, is usually of a much coarser quality, both as regards the glaze and the decoration, than any of the other forms of English Delft, from which there is but little difficulty in distinguishing it. In the first place the backs of these pieces, principally plates, are usually covered with a yellowish lead glaze, applied for the purpose of concealing the innumerable perforations which would otherwise disfigure the under portion. The decoration, again, ranges itself in great measure under the heads of very rude representations of Adam and Eve (a speciality of the Staffordshire potter), and of portraits of contemporary celebrities, King William and Queen Mary, Queen Anne, George I., the Duke of Marlborough, &c. The glaze is of a yellowish cast, the figures sketched in a most hasty and conventional manner, the colouring largely of yellow, blue, and green, of the most inartistic kind; trees are dabbed in with a sponge, and one glance at these big plates, intended no doubt for the decoration of walls and dressers, gives the impression that the artist was paid by the dozen. We have mentioned these portrait pieces for the purpose of identification, but, for reasons given in the Introduction, they do not come within our scope.

1680. (No. 534.) A circular Dish; decorated in blue and yellow, outlined in lake, with figures of two workmen seated at a table in an open landscape, examining border designs for dishes; the master appears coming forward in the distance. Inscribed with initials and date—

S 1680
·:· W·:·E·:·

Diameter 16½ *in.*
COLL. LATE *W.E.*

1686. (No. 535.) A Dish; decorated with a large crown in centre in yellow and blue, inscribed below with date in blue, with border on edge of flowers and scrolls.

1686

Diameter 13 *in.* COLL. *J.F.*

1691. (No. 536.) A Dish, similar to above; decorated with a large crown in centre, in yellow and blue, and inscribed below with date in blue, with pattern on edge, of flowers and insects, rudely washed in in yellow and blue.

1691

Diameter 12½ *in.* COLL. *J.F.*

1718. (No. 537.) A Plate; glazed at the back with lead-bluish glaze, decorated in blue; good floral ornament around large square, in which is the alphabet in Roman letters. Inscribed on the inside rim with initials and date. Possibly decorated by a Dutch artist.

TPB:1718.

Diameter 8¾ *in.* COLL. *J.E.H.*

A large number of Earthenware Gravestones is in existence, inscribed with names and dates, which it would be impossible to enumerate.

UNCERTAIN DELFT.

1649. (No. 538.) A Dish; decorated with coat of arms, and inscribed with name and date—

Sold by Cadd

anno *domini*

16 49

Diameter 15 *in.* Coll. *H.W.*

1663. (No. 539.) A large Dish; decorated in colours with ship and floral border; the back yellow. Inscribed with initials and date—

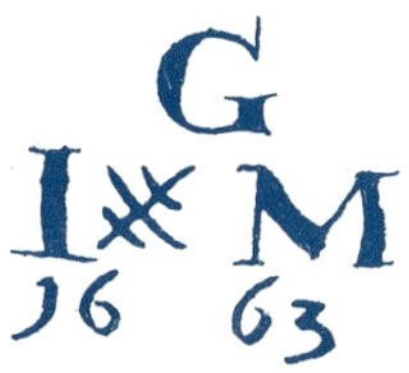

Diameter 22 *in.*
B. Mus. (*Franks Coll.*).

1670. (No. 540.) A Dish; decorated with the Weavers' arms, and inscribed with initials and date. The back yellow.

C

B · E

1670

Diameter 16 *in.*
Coll. *Earl of Mt. E.*

1673. (No. 541.) A Dish, of uncertain fabric; decorated with a vase of flowers, in colours. Inscribed with initials and date—

K
I · M
1673

Diameter $19\frac{1}{2}$ *in.*
COLL. EARL OF MT. E.

1681. (No. 542.) A Dish; decorated with a figure of Fortune seated on a globe in the centre, a coat of arms on each side. Inscribed with initials and date—

H · M · A · M · E · W · 1681 ·

Diameter 13 *in.*

1681. (No. 543.) A Jug; decorated with the Triumph of Neptune and Amphitrite, and coat of arms above; pewter lid; inscribed with initials and date—

W · R 1681

1705. (No. 544.) A Plate; decorated in blue, and inscribed with initials and date—

· H
· I ·:· M ·
· J705 ·

Diameter $8\frac{5}{8}$ *in.* COLL. J.H.

1715. (No. 545.) A circular Dish; decorated in the centre with cartouche containing inscription and date—

Thomas and Elesebath Kockerill
Bridlington Quay 1715

Diameter $13\frac{1}{2}$ *in.* COLL. T.B.

1728. (No. 546.) A Dish; inscribed in blue with initials and date—

A·:·F
1728

Diameter $7\frac{3}{4}$ *in.*
B. Mus. (*Franks Coll.*).

1728. (No. 547.) A Bowl; inscribed on the inside with motto and date—

Drink faire
Dont Sware
1728

Height $6\frac{1}{2}$ *in.*; *diameter* $11\frac{1}{2}$ *in.*
B. Mus.
(*Willett Coll.*).

1734. (No. 547A.) A Bowl; ornamented on the outside with six panels of conventional flowers, in blue. Inscribed on the bottom of bowl on the inside—

Drink fair
Dont Spear
1734

underneath the bowl—
IX A
3

Height 5 *in.*; *diameter* 9 *in.*
Coll. Lord W.

1743. (No. 548.) A Dish or Tray, with six-lobed edge, supported on seven small feet; painted in central hexagonal panel with tea-drinking scene in a room. Inscribed in blue with initials and date—

17:E+A:43

Coll. M.P.G.

1753. (No. 549.) A Plate; decorated with arms—chevron, between three cocks. Inscribed with initials and date on back—

T + M
1753

Diameter 9 *in.*
B. Mus. (*Franks Coll.*).

1753. (No. 550.) A Plate, exactly similar to No. 549. Inscribed with initials and date—

T + M
1753

Diameter 9 *in.*
B. Mus. (*Franks Coll.*).

1753. (No. 551.) A Tablet; mentioned by Miss Meteyard in her "Life of Wedgwood." Decorated in the centre with a coat of arms in blue. Inscribed on each side with an initial, and below with date—

T. E.
1753

1754. (No. 552.) A Bowl, painted in colours; outside, a landscape; inside, shepherd in landscape, under which inscription and date—

Richard Wyatt; Appelsham
Prosperety to the Flock
May th30; 1754

Height 6 *in.*; *diameter* 14 *in.* *B. Mus.* (*Willett Coll.*).

1768. (No. 553.) A Tea-Poy; greyish-blue ground, decorated in dark blue with rough floral ornament. Inscribed on two sides with names and date—

Chriftopher Stonlake, Marjey Stonlake
1768

Height $4\frac{1}{4}$ *in.*; *diameter* $3\frac{1}{4}$ *in.*

1770. (No. 554.) A Puzzle-Jug (broken). Inscribed with motto—

Within this Cup there is good liquor
Fit for Parson or for Vicar
But how to drink and not to spill
Will tax the utmost of your skill

Height 6 *in.; diameter* 3 *in.* COLL. *H.W.*

UNCERTAIN DELFT, UNDATED.

(No. 555.) A Dish; decorated with the portrait of the Duke of Marlborough, and inscribed with initials—

D. M.

Diameter 13 *in.*
COLL. *L.M.S.*

DUTCH DELFT CONNECTED WITH ENGLAND.

IT has been thought desirable to include in this work a few specimens which, though of Continental origin, are in various ways connected with this country. An additional reason for this course is that some of them have been erroneously attributed in several works to an English source. For instance, Marryat (3rd ed., p. 226) gives as having been made at Lowestoft the two Quinton plates (B.M.). They are also attributed to this fabrique by Chaffers (4th ed., p. 833), as well as the dish upon which are inscribed the names of Robert and Ann Parrish. The frequent presence of Dutch ware in the Eastern Counties is accounted for by their close commercial connection with Holland, a notable illustration of which is to be found in the nomenclature of Delft Street, in Sandwich.

On examining the make of the specimens it will be seen that they differ from English and resemble Dutch examples, certain peculiarities in the inscriptions pointing also in the same direction; for example, the mark over the letter *u* to distinguish it from *n*, and the two dots over the *y*, which were not in use in England. There are also mistakes in spelling the names, possible only to a foreigner. With these may be associated the plates painted at Delft by Sir James Thornhill, as shown by the inscriptions on the reverse, verified by the mention in his Diary of his presence in Holland in the year 1711 (the date inscribed upon the plates). It is possible that the formal borders were painted by one of the Dutch potters, and that Sir James confined his attention to decorating the plates with the signs of the Zodiac.

We must, however, confess that pieces of indisputable Lambeth origin, *e.g.*, Nos. 311 and 312, exhibit some of the same characteristics; the explanation unquestionably being that the *inscriptions* on these pieces were executed by foreign workmen living in England.

It is a well-known fact in the history, not only of this ware, but also of White Salt-glazed Earthenware, that German or Dutch artists were employed in the decoration. The necessity for the discrimination above alluded to is evidenced with especial clearness by an inspection of No. 556, where we observe a peculiarity which would at the first glance stamp it as essentially English. We refer to the arrangement of the initial letters in a cartouche on the margin of the plate. These unquestionably indicate the initials of the possessor and his wife; the uppermost standing for the surname, and the lower for their respective Christian names. This fashion runs through the whole series of the

English tokens of the 17th century, and has usually been considered as characteristic of English work. But, in the present instance, not only are the style and colour of decoration, the body, and the glaze un-English in character, but the mark at the back, reproduced in the text, is the well-known mark of a Dutch potter.

1696. (No. 556.) A large circular Plate; beautifully decorated with birds, flowers, etc., in blue of a darker shade than that generally used in Lambeth Delft. Inscribed on the margin, in the English fashion, with initials, and bearing on the back a mark, mentioned by Chaffers as being that of a Dutch potter, but he has not identified the name or given the date.

Diameter 16 *in.*
COLL. *J.E.H.*

1711. (No. 557.) Twelve Plates; painted at Delft, in Holland, by Sir James Thornhill, in the year 1711. The designs, which are beautifully executed, represent the twelve signs of the Zodiac, and have at the back the conventional mark of each. The borders probably painted by an inferior artist.

J. Thornhill. fi
Delph Aug. 1711.

1711. (No. 558 and No. 559.) The Taurus and Virgo of the set above described.

1740. (No. 560.) A circular Plate; decorated in blue with conventional border, and inscribed in the centre (within a florid cartouche surrounded by three fishes) with names and date—

Diameter 9½ *in.*
Coll. J.S.

An exactly similar specimen. *Diameter* 8¾ *in.* *B. Mus.* (*Franks Coll.*).

1752. (No. 561.) Two circular Plates, of coarse paste; decorated with blue borders, and inscribed in the centre with names and date—

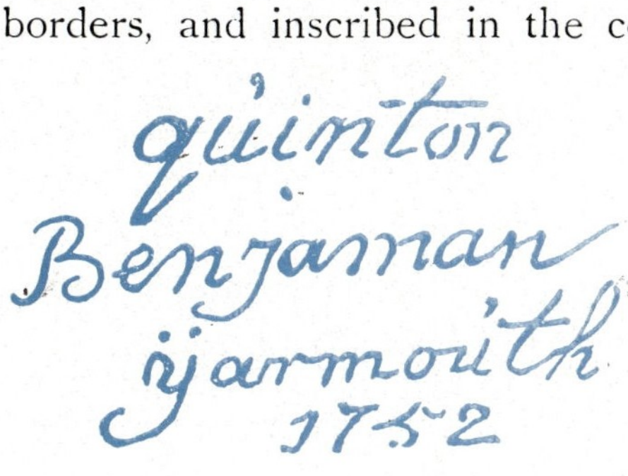

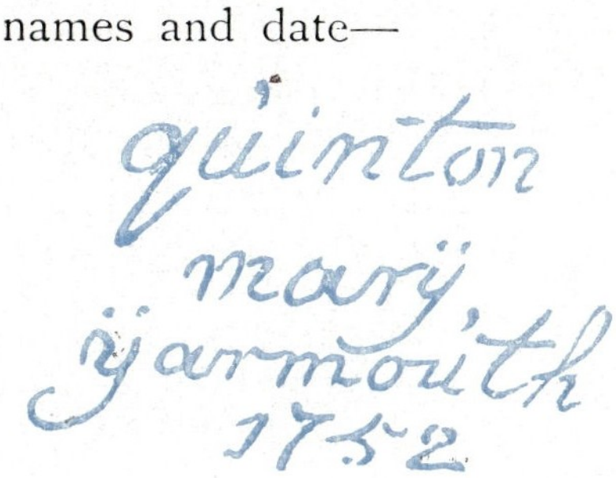

B. Mus. (*Franks Coll.*).

1754. (No. 562.) A circular Dish; decorated in blue with a bold border round the rim, the centre bearing a heart-shaped cartouche, inscribed with names and date, and surmounted with a coronet—

William and
Suanna Plumer
Yarmouth
1754

Coll. B. Mus.

1756. (No. 563.) A remarkably fine blue and white circular Dish, similar to the above, Inscribed in the same manner.

Robart & Ann
Parrish
in Norwich
1756

B. Mus. (Franks Coll.).

1757. (No. 564.) A circular Dish; similar to the above specimens, and inscribed in the same manner.

Iohn : & Dorethey
Woolstone
Harwich
1757

Diameter 12 *in.* *Coll. J.E.H.*

(No. 565.) A large Bowl; decorated in blue with pattern of conventional flowers and small border. Inscribed in front, on a kind of label, with name and address, and marked on bottom with initials of maker. The mark is given by Chaffers as that of a Dutch potter, but he has not identified the name nor given a date.

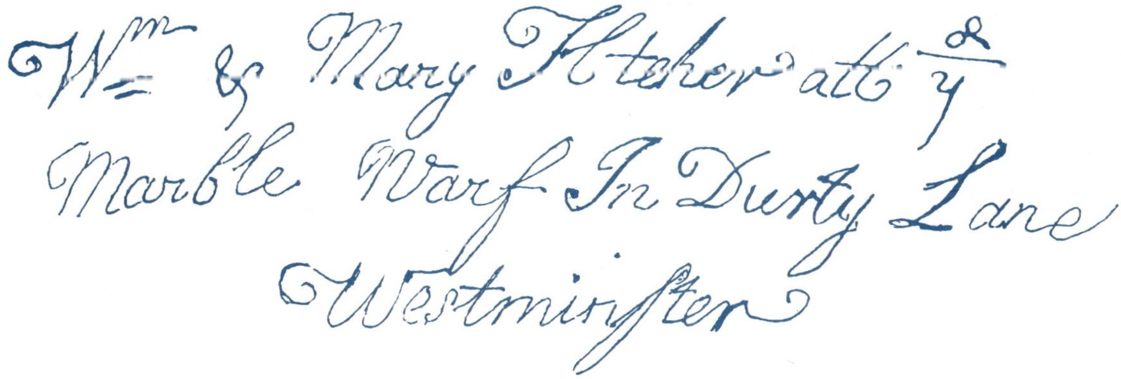

Diameter 14 *in.* *Coll. B. Mus.*

WHITE SALT-GLAZE.

THIS charming ware carries in its face credentials, not only, for the most part, to its character as one of the most beautiful of all English Ceramic productions, but also to its identity. After a short practice it is impossible not to recognise its peculiar glaze—not even and spread as is the case with all other glazes, but granular, and yet smooth as a whole—compared with justice by some writers to the surface of a lemon, its colour, however, being white, drab, or grey, nearer as a rule to that of *putty* than any other familiar substance. The body is extremely hard, and brittle when exposed to hot water. The decoration is very varied, whether moulded, incised, scratched, or embossed. The scratched patterns are frequently tinted with blue, enamel colours and gilding being freely applied to the more elaborate pieces. Want of space prevents anything like a full enumeration of the forms which this ware assumes, many of them being fanciful and artistic in a high degree; but tea-pots, sauce-boats, cups, jugs, bowls, plates, tea-poys, vases, figures of men and animals, are among those most frequently met with. The earliest dated piece which we record is inscribed 1701, and the quaintest, perhaps, No. 570 in our own collection, is dated 1749; but, as indicated in the Introduction, there is a great dearth of dated or inscribed pieces in this ware.

1701. (No. 566.) A Mug; decorated with two bands of excellent ornament, and a medallion in relief. Inscribed with date.

Coll. M.I.H.

1724. (No. 567.) A Bottle or Flask; decorated on one side with initials and date, and incised into the ware, and coloured dark brown, On the other side a bird and foliage, also incised and coloured dark brown. An early specimen of dated Salt-Glaze.

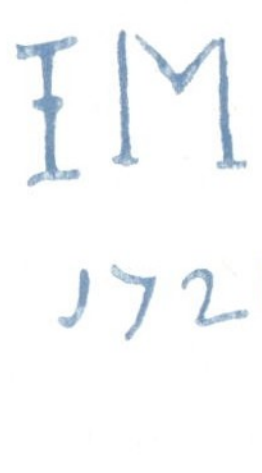

Height $3\frac{3}{4}$ *in.; diameter* $3\frac{1}{8}$ *in.*

Coll. B. Mus., late W.E.

1747. (No. 568.) A Mug; white, decorated in blue with turned lines. Inscribed and dated on one side—

William : Ball :
1747

Height 5 *in.*; *diameter* 4¼ *in.*
SCHREIBER COLL.

1748. (No. 569.) A Posset-Pot, with two handles; inscription and date incised in blue on both sides.

George Wall 1748 — *Elizabeth Wall* 1748

Height 9 *in.*; *diameter* 9 *in.* COLL. *H.W.*

1749. (No. 570.) A large Mug; decorated in the centre with figure of a man holding an axe; on one side a bull, on the other side flowers and foliage. Inscribed with name and date. All incised in the ware, and the incision painted in with dark blue.

John Cope 1749
Ucar gous

Height 6 *in.* COLL. *J.E.H.*, LATE *W.E.*

1750. (No. 571.) A Cup, with two handles; plain white, with incised inscription—

Mary Cowdal
of Frolesworth : 1750

Height 4½ *in.*; *diameter* 5 *in.*
COLL *B. M.*

1752. (No. 572.) A Mug; decorated with flowers and leaves, and a wreath enclosing initials and date, scratched in blue; narrow border in the same colour, of herring-bone pattern. *Height* 5 *in.* *S. K. Mus.* (SCHREIBER COLL.).

I H
1752

1755. (No. 573.) A Two-handled cylindrical Cup; decorated, with incised lines filled in with blue, with bird and flowers. Inscribed with initials and date—

Height $3\frac{3}{4}$ *in.*
B. Mus. (*Willett Coll.*).

1757. (No. 574.) A Two-handled Bowl; inscribed with initials and date—

Height $7\frac{3}{4}$ *in.; diameter* $8\frac{1}{2}$ *in.*
Coll. H.W.

1758. (No 575.) A cylindrical Mug; inscription and date in front; below are the rose and thistle, and above a narrow formal border, all scratched in the clay, and coloured a pale blue.

This is Thomas Cox'es Cup:
Come my friend and Drink it Vp.
Good News is come'n the Bells do Ring
& here's a health to Prussia's King
February 16*th* 1758

Height $5\frac{5}{8}$ *in; diameter* 6 *in.*
S. K. Mus. (*Schreiber Coll.*).

1759. (No. 576.) A Bottle; decorated with festoons and bouquets of flowers and birds moulded in relief; silver mount to neck. Inscribed with incised initials and date. The date appears to have been originally 1758, and to have been altered.

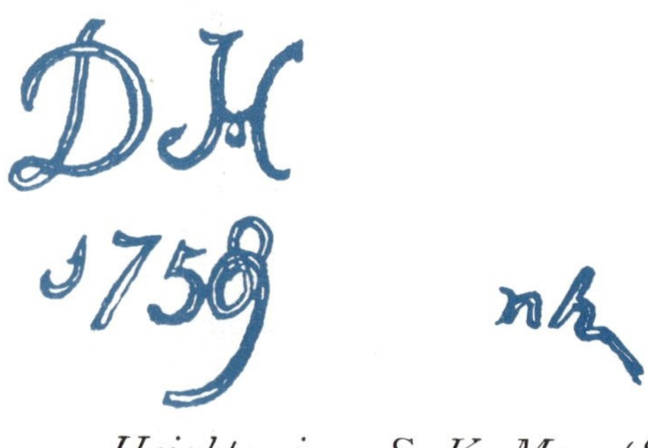

Height 9 *in.* *S. K. Mus.* (*Schreiber Coll.*).

1761. (No. 577.) A Jug, with incised blue floral decoration. Inscribed in script with name and date—

Martha Mason
July 23^{d} 1761

Height $5\frac{1}{8}$ *in.; diameter* 3 *in.*

COLL. *J.E.H.*

1763. (No. 578.) A Punch-Bowl; decorated, in colours, with figures of a lady and gentlemen on one side, and a country-girl on the other. Inscribed on the inside with motto—

ONE BOWL MORE AND THEN

and on the outside in black with name and date—

Iohn Bullock
1763

COLL. *DR. B.*

1763. (No. 579.) A large oval Soup-Tureen, Cover, and Stand. Body decorated with moulded ornament, including scroll-work and diaper and basket patterns; the tureen mounted on three lion's claws with masks. On the inside of the cover the initials *J.B.* have been rudely scratched in cursive letters while the paste was soft, and the letters subsequently covered with the glaze. Inscribed in a similar manner at the bottom of tureen with initials and date—

J.B. 1763.

COLL. *M.P.G.*

1766. (No. 580.) A circular Pocket-Flask; inscribed with date.

Coll. L.M.S.

1767. (No. 581.) A Jug; ornamented with incised scrolls, flowers, etc., tinted with blue. Inscribed with name and date—

T. Syms. 1767

Height 9 in. *Coll. late R.H.S.-S.*

1776. (No. 582.) A Mug; decorated in blue with figure of St. George and the Dragon. Inscribed in script with name and date—

A . Dunn Birminghame 1776

Height $4\frac{1}{2}$ in.; diameter $3\frac{1}{8}$ in. *Coll. H.W.*

1778. (No. 583.) A Tea-Pot and Cover. Body globose, mounted on foot, and painted in colours with a ship and flowers, and inscribed with initials and date—

I. B. 1778

Height 7 in. *Coll. M.P.G.*

WHITE SALT-GLAZE, UNDATED.

(No. 584.) A beautiful hexagonal Tea-Pot, with Cover; of Oriental character, decorated with numerous figures and with foliage. The six panels bear the following incised inscriptions, explanatory of the designs: (1) Old Vice Roy of Kanton; (2) Ambassadors of Lammas; (3) Round Pepper; (4) G·R·A·N·D·TARTAR·HAM·CHINA·; (5) China Root; (6) Young Vice Roy of Canton.

Coll. S. Mus.

(No. 585.) A Puzzle-Jug, of elegant form; inscription in incised blue in floral wreath—

MH

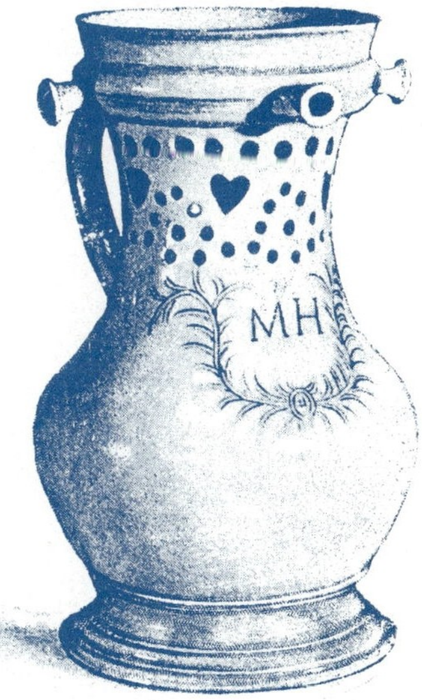

Height $7\frac{1}{2}$ *in.; diameter* $4\frac{1}{2}$ *in.*

Coll. J.E.H.

(No. 586.) A Two-handled Goblet; inscription in floral border, incised in blue; incised blue floral decoration at back.

Remember me
When this you see
Tho many mils
We distant be.

Height 5 *in.; diameter* $4\frac{1}{2}$ *in.*

Coll. J.E.H.

(No. 587.) A Punch-Bowl; rudely decorated in colours with flowers and insects. Inscribed with motto—

ANOTHER BOWLE
AND THEN

Described by J.E.H.

(No. 588.) A Jug, with inscription in cursive characters, incised in blue—

Martha Steel

Described by J.E.H.

(No. 589.) A Pair of Plates, with wavy edges, and flowers moulded in relief, beautifully enamelled in rich colours; in the centre a garden scene with a shepherd piping; above, a large monogram in gold on a green ground; border of diaper, interrupted by panels with flowers.

Diameter $9\frac{1}{8}$ *in.*
SCHREIBER COLL., *also* COLL. *J.E.H.*

(No. 590.) A Jug; decorated with garden-party scene, and bearing inscription—

Succefs to Mr.
John Calverly
of Leeds

Height $7\frac{1}{2}$ *in.*

(Mr. Calverly was three times Mayor of Leeds.) COLL. LATE *W.E.*

(No. 591.) A very fine Mug; decorated with a portrait of George II., surrounded with seven coats of arms, six of them belonging to Staffordshire families, viz., Hales-Baronet, Leveson-Gower, Vane and Bertie, Whorewood and Granville. Bearing inscription—

God save King George
and my Master.

Height 7 in. COLL. *L.M.S.*

(No. 592.) A Quart Jug; decorated with rather poor floral decoration. Inscription in large cartouche—

SUCCESS TO THE POST CHAISE DRIVER.

Height $8\frac{1}{8}$ in.; diameter 4 in. Described by J.E.H.

(No. 593.) A bell-shaped Mug; decorated with incised lines, filled in with blue. Bearing inscription—

Wenman and Dashwood. Old Interest for Ever
no double Return

Height $3\frac{1}{2}$ in. B. Mus. (Willett Coll.);
also 5 in. high and 3 in. wide. Coll. H.W.

(No. 594.) A Mug; decorated with rude border and inscription. Incised in blue—

Sir William a Plumper.

Coll. L. Mus.

In 1761 Liverpool was the scene of a strongly contested election between three rival candidates, viz., Sir William Meredith, Bart., Sir Ellis Cuncliffe, Bart., and Charles Pole, Esq., and the election was carried by the potters, 102 of whom gave plumpers for Sir William.

(No. 595.) A Mug; decorated with floral pattern, incised in blue; and inscribed with initials enclosed within wreath—

I L

Coll. L.M.S.

(No. 596.) A Jug, with straight lip; decorated, in enamel colours, with a panel enclosing a portrait of the Young Pretender in a tartan dress, and the initials P.C.; on each side a red rose and a thistle with green leaves; round the edge, inner and outer, border of diaper pattern.

Height $8\frac{1}{4}$ in. S. K. Mus. (Schreiber Coll.).

(No. 597.) A Jug, with straight lip; enamelled in colours; in front are two men, one of them holding an umbrella, the other, in a bright yellow dress, carrying a basket; beyond, flowers in a vase, etc.; narrow border of diaper pattern. Under the handle the letter B is inscribed in black.

Height 5 *in.* *S. K. Mus.* (*Schreiber Coll.*).

(No. 598.) A Jug; inscribed on the lower part, beneath the lip, with name in black; decorated with large bouquets of roses and other flowers in enamel colours, and three beaded borders, coloured.

Thos Allsop.

Height $8\frac{3}{4}$ *in.* *S. K. Mus.* (*Schreiber Coll.*).

(No. 599.) A Jug, with straight lip, below which is a panel enclosing inscription; on each side, a rose and green leaves enamelled in colours.

LIBERTY AND PROPERTY
NO EXCISE.

Height $6\frac{3}{4}$ *in.* *S. K. Mus.* (*Schreiber Coll.*).

The popularity of this motto dates from the year 1733, when Sir Robert Walpole's obnoxious Excise Bill was abandoned.

(No. 600.) A Pair of oblong Tea-Poys; on each side, a tea-plant and narrow upper border, moulded in low relief; in front, the inscription—

C I A
or T E
herb

on the reverse— Herb Tea.

Height $3\frac{3}{4}$ *in.* *S. K. Mus.* (*Schreiber Coll.*).

FULHAM BROWN STONEWARE.

THIS interesting and frequently picturesque ware belongs to the same family as the White Salt-glazed vessels, owing, as it does, its surface to the presence of salt in vapour in the kiln. Being made of coarser material, and in ruder forms, it possesses but little of artistic feeling, but the quaint figures usually embossed on its surface give it a rough charm of its own. It is mostly found in the form of mugs and tankards; jugs and bottles resembling the foreign Bellarmines are of less frequent occurrence. Fulham Brown Stoneware was in fact a survival, on the same premises, of the celebrated Dwight Pottery, a few noble relics from which alone remain to tantalise us. The talented founder of the pottery having been gathered to his fathers (the De Witts, first of Holland, then of Oxfordshire, finally of Fulham), and the models, tools, and moulds used by him having been hidden or destroyed, his successors were left to make vessels as best they might for daily use. The hunting-scenes, copies of a portion of Hogarth's Midnight Modern Conversation, figures of St. George and the Dragon, and the head of Queen Anne, embossed on this ware, are familiar to collectors, and now and then we get a date or name. Perhaps the most interesting specimen of this ware known is No. 614, Coll. H.C.M., a large mug, inscribed "*Walter Vaughan of Hereford, His Mugg must not be brock* 1740." The earliest dated example we have seen is No. 601, Coll. J.E.H., dated 1721.

1721. (No. 601.) A Mug; decorated with a ship and figure of a shipwright caulking the seams of the hull. Inscribed in script with name and date—

Robert Asslet
17 London Street 21

Height $8\frac{1}{4}$ *in.; diameter* $5\frac{1}{2}$ *in.*

Coll. J.E.H.

1724. (No. 602.) A Mug; decorated in front with sign of a sugarloaf, and inscribed in script with name and date—

Alex^d. Paterſon. In King Harry Yard 1724

Height $6\frac{3}{4}$ *in.; diameter* $4\frac{1}{4}$ *in.* *B. Mus.* (*Franks Coll.*).

1724–5. (No. 603.) A Mug; decorated with bust of Queen Anne, a church, two men with guns, head of King Charles in oak; below a coursing scene; inscription and date round edge—

On Bansted downs a hare was found
Which Led us all a smoking round.
Abraham Harman at Lewis in Suſsex 1724–5.

(*See also* Nos. 607, 608.) *Height* $8\frac{3}{8}$ *in.; diameter* $5\frac{1}{2}$ *in.*
B. Mus. (*Willett Coll.*).

1727. (No. 604.) A Mug; decorated with portrait of Queen Anne, halberdier, running dogs, &c., and inscribed in script with name and date—

Thomas Johnson
1727

Height 8 *in.*
Coll. L.M.S.

1727. (No. 605.) A large Mug; decorated with rude figures in low relief, representing stag-hunting, shooting, wrestling, and other country sports; inscribed in script with name and date—

Edw. Slark, 1727

Coll. M.P.G.

1729. (No. 606.) A Mug, of grey ware, partially coloured with brown; decorated in the front with medallion of Queen Anne, and inscribed with legend and date in script—

Drink to the pious Memmory of good Queen Anne
1729 *Coll. L.M.S.*

1729. (No. 607.) A cylindrical Tankard; decorated with various subjects in relief; in front a bust of Queen Anne, and on each side a Yeoman of the Guard; detached formal roses and trees; below a hunting-scene, and name inscribed; legend and date round the rim; pewter mount.

On Banse downs a haur wee found
thatt led us all a Smoaking Round
1729
Wm. Marsh

Height 9 *in.; diameter* 5½ *in.*
S. K. Mus. (*Schreiber Coll.*).

1730. (No. 608.) A Mug; decorated with bust of Queen Anne, two beef-eaters, a church, two Boscobel oaks, and below a hunting-scene. Inscribed with legend and date in script—

Drink about Boys to the Pious
Memory of Queen Anne.
Mary Bayley, 1730

Height 8½ *in.; diameter* 5½ *in.*
Coll. W.M.

1731. (No. 609.) A Mug; similar to above in Schreiber Coll. Inscribed round the rim with legend and date—

on Banestead Downs a hare was found
which led us all a smoaking Round 1731

Height 8⅜ *in.; diameter* 6⅜ *in.*
Coll. J.E.H.

1734. (No. 610.) A Mug; decorated in the usual style with portrait of Queen Anne, beefeaters, and hunting-scene; inscribed round the rim with legend and date in script—

Come Let us Drink to the Pious Memomery of Good Queen Ann
1734

Height 7½ *in.* Coll. F.B.

1735. (No. 611.) A fine Tankard, with handle; decorated with spirited stag-hunting scene, a man on horse and one on foot; above this an *appliqué* plaque in low relief shows a stag-hunt on much smaller scale. On one side of the plaque is coat of arms, and name and date inscribed in script—

Jno. and Ann Nicholas . 1735

Coll. G. Mus.

1735. (No. 612.) A Jug, bearing inscription and date—

Thos. Foord at the Catts, Lewis, Sufsex. 1735.

Height 7¼ *in.; diameter* 4¾ *in.* Coll. H.W.

1739. (No. 613.) A Tankard; decorated with subjects in relief, a stag-hunt—huntsmen, hounds, and stag—among which are birds and trees, and inscription and date—

Southwell for Ever . *J.H.*

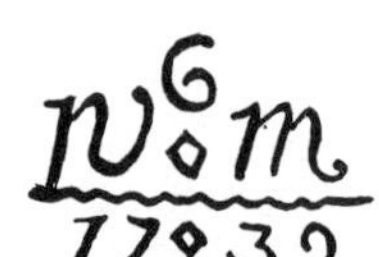

Above and below a border of rosettes and lozenges. On the bottom is scratched—

John Harwell

Height 10 *in.; diameter* 7 *in.* S. K. Mus. (Schreiber Coll.).

1740. (No. 614.) A very large Mug with pewter mount; decorated in the centre with a medallion representing Hogarth's "Midnight Modern Conversation"; on the left and right of this two smaller subjects—a stag-hunt, and a bull tied by the horns with a man standing over him with axe in hand. A legend runs round the centre of the mug; immediately below the medallion is a shield bearing the Old Butchers' arms of Hereford, and below this the date.

Waller Vaughan of Hereford
His mugg must not be brock 1740.

Height $15\frac{3}{8}$ *in.; diameter* 6 *in.* COLL. *H.C.M.*

1743. (No. 615.) A Mug; decorated with a highly embossed figure of St. George and the Dragon, of very archaic type, on a raised plaque in front of mug. Inscribed in script with name and date. Small excise mark, impressed G R and crown.

Thomas Cupett
1743

Height $6\frac{1}{2}$ *in.; diameter* $4\frac{1}{2}$ *in.*
COLL. *J.E.H.*

1747. (No. 616.) A large Jug; decorated with medallion containing portrait, and hunting-scene. Inscribed with name and date—

Wm. Wright 1747

Height $12\frac{1}{2}$ *in.; diameter* 9 *in.* COLL. *H.W.*

1752. (No. 617.) A Mug; decorated with hunting-scene and medallion containing Hogarth's "Midnight Modern Conversation." Inscribed in script with name and date—

Francis Salt. 1752

Height 8 *in.; diameter* 7½ *in.* COLL. *A.E.C.*

1761. (No. 618.) A Mug; decorated with various subjects in relief; in front, a square tablet containing Hogarth's "Midnight Modern Conversation"; on one side a house and trees; on the reverse a table with two busts, under which an inscription; below, a stag-hunt and name and date.

Wee three Loggerheads
G. Ieffrey. 1761

Height 8½ *in.; diameter* 5 *in.*
S. K. MUS. (SCHREIBER COLL.).

1761. (No. 619.) A Mug, similar to No. 615, but the figures of St. George and the Dragon less quaintly designed. Inscription impressed by punches; small excise mark, impressed, W.P.

Alex^r Ballantine
Twickenham
1761.

Height 6¾ *in.; diameter* 4¼ *in.*
COLL. *J.E.H.*

1762. (No. 620.) A Mug, with incised inscription and date—

Thos. Mafon, Burntwood. 1762.

1763. (No. 621.) A small cylindrical Mug; decorated on one side with pattern of rose and leaves, on the other inscription and date. Found in Nottingham on removing soil from land formerly property of the Wyer family.

John Wyer. 1763.

Height $3\frac{1}{2}$ *in.; diameter* 3 *in.* COLL. *S.K.*

1763. (No. 622.) A Mug; decorated on the lower part with stag-hunting scene; above, a stage-waggon, drawn by six horses in file, waggoner, and man on horseback; on each side of handle a shield with lion rampant. Inscribed with impressed lettering—

Lionel and Ann Pepper, Ipswich. 1763.

Height 8 *in.; diameter* $5\frac{1}{2}$ *in.* COLL. *T.B.*

1764. (No. 623.) A Quart Mug; decorated in the front with drinking-scene in low relief, and hunting-scene below, and inscribed with name and date—

William Heath. 1764

Height 9 *in.; diameter* $5\frac{1}{2}$ *in.* *Described by J.E.H.*

FULHAM STONEWARE, UNDATED.

(No. 624.) A Brown Jug, with narrow neck; of the same shape as the Bellarmine jugs, but without mask; decorated in front with medallion containing figure of a cock, and inscribed with initials—

H·C

Height $8\frac{1}{2}$ *in.; diameter* $4\frac{3}{4}$ *in.*
COLL. *J.E.H.*

An almost exactly similar specimen in the Mayer Museum, Liverpool, has the initials—

T·D

(No. 625.) A Pint Jug, of the usual Fulham ware; under a crown, in relief, an impressed inscription—

Brill House
St Pancras

This is an interesting specimen of a public-house measure. The Inn, now rebuilt, is called by Malcolm "a comfortable country tavern," and is mentioned by Stukeley, who supposed it to be named from a "Bury Hill" of the Romans (an erroneous conjecture); many old drawings of it exist. There seems, we think, to be no reasonable doubt that it received its name somewhere about 1690, and that it was a Whig reminder of the *Brill* (mouth of the Meuse), from which the Prince of Orange sailed in defence (among other things) of the Protestant religion. The crown favours this suggestion

COLL. *J.E.H.*

(No. 626.) A very large grey Stoneware Jug; decorated at the top with impressed medallions, suggesting the cure of the gout by draughts of the contents.

Iron Peartree Water
near Godstone
Surry

Height $13\frac{3}{4}$ *in.; Diameter* 9 *in.*
COLL. *J.E.H.;*
also B. MUS. (*WILLETT* COLL.).

(No. 627.) A Flip-Can, mentioned by Mr. Jewitt; bearing incised inscription—

Alexander Selkirke. This is my one
When you take me on board of Ship
Pray fill me full with punch or flipp
Fulham.

This Jug, which belonged to "Robinson Crusoe," was obtained from the Fulham Pottery about the year 1703, whilst waiting for the equipment and sailing of the Cinque Ports Galley, to which he had been appointed sailing-master, and doubtless accompanied him on his voyage to Juan Fernandez; it was highly venerated in his family, and kept locked up for fifty years by one of his nieces.

(No. 628.) A cylindrical Pint Mug; brown above and buff below, of exactly similar character to No. 610. Handle broken off; embossed bust of Queen Anne (crowned), also inscription—

To the pyouse Memory of
Good Queen Ann
Thos. Squier

Height $4\frac{7}{8}$ *in.; diameter* $3\frac{1}{2}$ *in.* COLL. G. MUS.

(No 629.) A Mug; decorated in front with the sign of an angel; stamped inscription—

James Kemp

Height $3\frac{1}{2}$ *in.; diameter* $2\frac{3}{4}$ *in.* COLL. B. MUS.

Nottingham, Brampton or Chesterfield.

THE Stonewares of Nottingham, Brampton or Chesterfield are also members of the great Brown Salt-glaze family, and have played a most important part in the history of our domestic drinking-vessels. After a short acquaintance with them it is easy to assign to each its proper source. Nottingham ware has a peculiar smoothness of surface and almost metallic lustre, which, when the eye has become familiar with it, is a ready help in distinguishing it from other wares; its decoration, instead of being embossed like that of Fulham and Lambeth, is incised in floral patterns—the most usual flower being a carnation—and scrolls, often cheered by birds. The most familiar shapes are those of jugs, mugs, two-handled cups, and "bear-jugs." The latter, being undated and uninscribed, do not concern our present work. Brampton or Chesterfield Stoneware differs but slightly from Nottingham ware, but it is usually less hard and thicker, and not so well potted; the glaze is slightly iridescent, the decoration not so good as that of Nottingham, consisting to a large extent of bands of lineal and dotted work. Altogether this ware is, as a rule, clumsier and less attractive than that of its fellow, but they are often confounded, and it is quite possible to make mistakes in their attribution.

The same may most certainly be said of Lambeth Stoneware as contrasted with that of Fulham. Men apprenticed at the latter factory worked at the former, and the traditions of the pottery on the Middlesex side of the river were doubtless respected at those on the opposite bank, destined in time to tower head and shoulders above their parent. The majority of the old jugs decorated in relief with hunting- and drinking-scenes, which are familiar to this generation, owe their origin rather to Lambeth than to Fulham; the glaze of the latter appears, as a rule, to have been more brilliant than that of the earlier factory, and the brown colour which almost always occupies the upper portion of the vessel is generally of a richer tone. As is well known, the manufacture has been continued without a break since its commencement in the year 1751. The Pottery now in the hands of Messrs. Stiff & Sons seems to occupy, with large additions, the original site, which is said to have formed a portion of old Hereford House. The only dated piece of Lambeth Stoneware we have met with is illustrated and described on page 180, No. 670, Coll. J.E.H. This date, 1751, cannot be that at which the jug was made; the costume of the figures negatives the idea. It was probably potted towards the end of the last century, and the date and figure doubtless refer to the year in which the factory started, and to some well-known character employed therein. We have taken some trouble to investigate this point by reference to old employés, but without satisfactory result.

1700. (No. 630.) A Posset-Pot; the earliest known dated example of this ware, of the usual form, but fashioned with more than ordinary care and lightness; with a light-brown lustrous glaze; of a very unusual mode of construction, the "belly" part having double sides, the outer of which is ornamented with foliage and flowers, the stalks incised and the flowers and leaves perforated. A tube, commencing from the top, runs down the exterior side as far as the top of the "belly," where it passes through, and is continued to the bottom of the interior. Inscription and date on the front in cursive characters, and on the other side the royal arms of the period (Wm. III.), with crest, supporters, garter, and motto—

Samuel Watkinson Major
Sarah his Wife Majoress *of Nottingham*

I 7 O O

Described and illustrated by Mr. Jewitt, and assigned by him to the collection of Rev. J. S. Doxey.

1703. (No. 631.) A small Jug; brown glaze, the neck ribbed, the handle gadrooned, the outer body pierced with sprays of flowers, and incised with similar decoration and inscription; enclosing a smaller body. The bottom of the shell is open.

nott : 1703

Height $3\frac{7}{8}$ *in.; diameter* $3\frac{1}{2}$ *in.*

COLL. S. K. MUS.

1712. (No. 632.) A Jug; mentioned by Mr. Jewitt, bearing inscription inscribed in cursive letters—

John Smith junr. of Bassford near Nottingham
1712.

1720. (No. 633.) A Two-handled Cup; inscribed with date.
Height $3\frac{3}{4}$ *in.; diameter* $3\frac{1}{4}$ *in.* COLL. LATE *J.T.*

1720. (No. 634.) A Two-handled Cup, of fine shape; decorated with incised wreaths of foliage and flowers, and inscribed with date.
Height 8 *in.; diameter* 6 *in.* COLL. *J. HA.*

1721. (No. 635.) A Two-handled Pot; bellied, with horizontal indented band ornament joining the bottoms of the handles, and incised scroll ornament below. Incised inscription and date on the upper portion—

Henry Gibbens
And Ellin His Wife
June the 10th 1721

Height $9\frac{1}{4}$ *in.; diameter* $7\frac{3}{8}$ *in.*
On the other side 1721 within incised floral decoration. COLL. *J.E.H.*

1721. (No. 636.) A Mug; decorated with dragon and star, and inscribed in script with name and date—

Peter Waters, 1721.

Height 8 *in.; diameter* 5 *in.* COLL. *B. MUS.*

1726. (No. 637.) A Christening-Bowl; decorated with a double incised band round the rim and inscription in cursive characters—

Nouember 20. 1726 *Diameter* 13 *in.* COLL. *M.P.G.*

1746. (No. 638.) A large Cup or Jug, with two handles; inscribed in script with name and date—

John Buttler & Kathrine his Wife
June 11. 1746

Height $8\frac{1}{2}$ *in.; diameter* $8\frac{1}{8}$ *in.* COLL. *B. Mus.*

1747. (No. 639.) A Two-handled Cup, with horizontal indented band ornaments, and incised inscription and date—

Hannah Marsh
October the 22nd 1747

Height 8 *in.; diameter* $8\frac{1}{2}$ *in.* COLL. *J.E.H.*

1747. (No. 640.) A Punch-Bowl; light brown, decorated with purple flowers. Inscribed in script round foot—

Thomas & Elizabeth Whitehead. 1747

Height $7\frac{1}{2}$ *in.; diameter* $10\frac{1}{2}$ *in.* COLL. *Y. Mus.*

1747. (No. 641.) A Two-handled Cup; well decorated with incised patterns, consisting of concentric rings and bands, with a bold encircling wreath of conventional foliage. Inscribed in script with name and date—

Ann Goodwin, March 3*rd* 1747.

COLL. *W. P. Mus.*, SHEFFIELD.

1749. (No. 642.) A Mug; decorated round the middle with a band of diagonal lines, and inscribed above in script with name and date—

Mary Whates. April the 24*th* 1749

COLL. *N. C. Mus.*

1750. (No. 643.) A Punch-Bowl, of unusually large size; decorated with incised inscription in cursive characters—

Old England for Ever
1750.

Diameter 22 *in.*
COLL. *M.P.G.*

1752. (No. 644.) A Two-handled Cup; richly decorated, and inscribed with name and date in script—

Sarah Radford. Nott$^{m.}$ *March ye* 26 1752.

Height 9 *in.; diameter* $9\frac{1}{2}$ *in.* COLL. LATE *J.T.*

1753. (No. 645.) A Piece (?) mentioned by Mr. Jewitt. Inscribed and dated in script—

Thos. and Mary Brammer, May ye 21 1753.

1753. (No. 646.) A hexagonal Tea-Poy; inscribed with name and date in script—

mary more land nov^{m}

the 5th 1753 inscribed on bottom with initials— G F COLL. *L. Mus.*

1755. (No. 647.) A Puzzle-Jug, of graceful shape; decorated with incised conventional floral pattern, and inscribed in script in front with date, and bearing initials and date on bottom—

G= B
1755.

Height $8\frac{1}{2}$ *in.; Diameter* $5\frac{1}{4}$ *in.*
COLL. *N. C. Mus.*

1759. (No. 648.) A Two-handled Cup; decorated top and bottom with bands of crossed lines forming diamond pattern, and inscribed in the centre with names and date in script—

Thomas and Ann Lowe 1759

Height $9\frac{3}{4}$ *in.* COLL. *J.F.*

1760. (No. 649.) A large Jug; inscribed with names and date in script—

John and Elizabeth Townend
June 1st 1760

Height $10\frac{1}{4}$ *in.; diameter* $5\frac{3}{4}$ *in.*
COLL. *N. C. Mus.*

1760. (No. 650.) A Two-handled Cup; decorated with incised floral pattern, and inscribed with initials and date—

1760
E S.

Height 9 *in.; diameter* 8 *in.*
COLL. *J.F.*

1762. (No. 651.) A Mug; elaborately decorated in front with a device of roses and thistles surmounted by crowns; bearing at the back, on each side of the handle, an incised inscription and date. The bottom is also inscribed with the maker's name—

John / *Nottingham*
Johnſon / *Sepm ye* 3
Schoolmaster / 1762

On the bottom *Wm Lockett*

Height $8\frac{3}{4}$ *in.; diameter* 8 *in.*
COLL. *S.K.*

1765. (No. 652.) A Jar; decorated with slight impressed ornament, and date incised.

1766. (No. 653.) A Vessel in shape of Milk-Pail; inscribed with date incised.

Height $7\frac{1}{4}$ *in.; diameter* $8\frac{1}{2}$ *in.*

1767. (No. 654.) A Pepper-Box; slightly decorated, and inscribed with date.

Height 3 *in.; diameter* 3 *in.* COLL. LATE *J.T.*

1769. (No. 655.) A Ball; richly decorated, and inscribed with initials and date—

H. W. 1769.

Diameter $3\frac{1}{3}$ *in.* COLL. LATE *J.T.*

1769. (No. 656.) A Hollow Ball, intended probably for a child's rattle; very lustrous glaze, decorated with small pattern, and inscribed with name and date—

Elizabeth Clarck December ye 25th. 1769.

Diameter $3\frac{3}{4}$ *in.* COLL. LATE *W.S.*

1773. (No. 657.) A Two-handled Mug; decorated with incised ornament, and inscribed with names and date, also incised.

Thomas & Mary Sales, October 19th 1773.

Height 10 *in.; diameter* $8\frac{1}{2}$ *in.*

1781. (No. 658.) A Puzzle-Jug, with three spouts; very highly glazed, bearing incised inscription and date—

Edward Lernon, His Jug, 1781.

Height $7\frac{1}{2}$ *in.; diameter* $3\frac{1}{2}$ *in.* COLL. *F.B.*

1781. (No. 659.) A tall cylindrical Mug; decorated on one side with fine conventional floral ornament and bird, incised; and on the other side and along the bottom a lengthy inscription and date, also incised—

J. & E. Holland of Notts
made at Nottingham Feb. 16 1781.
Why may not this Poor Earthen
vessel hold as precious Lickuoir
as one Made of
GoLD

Height 9 *in.; diameter* $8\frac{1}{8}$ *in.* COLL. *N. C. Mus.*

1787. (No. 660.) A Two-handled Cup; decorated and inscribed with name and date—

John and Mary Rowbotham
Ot. 26. 1787

Height 10¼ *in.; diameter* 8½ *in.* COLL. LATE *J.T.*

1788. (No. 661.) A Puzzle-Jug; inscribed with legend and date—

Here Gentlemen come try your skill, &c.
Oct. 17. 1788.

Height 8 *in.; diameter* 5½ *in.* COLL. LATE *J.T.*

1790. (No. 662.) A Jug; decorated and inscribed with names and date. An old family relic, belonging to a relative of the late owner.

John Handforth, February the 5*th* 1790

Height 9¼ *in.; diameter* 7½ *in.* COLL. LATE *J.T.*

1791. (No. 663.) A Save-all; richly decorated, and inscribed with names and date—

John and Ann Sandum
January ye 5. 1791
J. A. S.

Height 7 *in.; diameter* 3⅔ *in.* COLL. LATE *J.T.*

1799. (No. 664.) A Puzzle-Jug; inscribed with date.

COLL. *L.M.S.*

1799. (No. 665.) A Pot for Salt; made in Nottingham, the initials being those of the wife of the maker. Dark brown, ornamented with slip decoration in white.

BRAMPTON OR CHESTERFIELD STONEWARE.

1749. (No. 666.) A large Two-handled Posset-Pot; decorated with incised ornament, and inscribed with name and date—

Robert Bruston
March the 2rd 1749
Derby

Height 8 *in.;* *diameter* $9\frac{1}{4}$ *in.*

1750. (No. 667.) A Two-handled Posset-Pot; decorated with incised floral pattern, and inscribed with date. Engraved and described in "The Reliquary," Vol. V. *Height* 7 *in.; diameter* 7 *in.* *Coll. J.H.*

1750. (No. 668.) A Two-handled Posset-Pot; decorated with incised floral pattern, and inscribed with date. Mentioned by Mr. Jewitt.

1774. (No. 669.) A Posset-Pot, made at Brampton; decorated with raised ornaments, and inscribed with date. Mentioned by Mr. Jewitt as being in the possession of Mr. J. G. Bagshawe.

LAMBETH STONEWARE.

1761. (No. 670.) A large Jug; very hard body, remarkably well potted; the relief ornament extremely sharp and finished by hand, glaze unusually dry.

Enlarged view of the seated figure.

Height $9\frac{1}{4}$ *in.; diameter* 7 *in.* *Coll. J.E.H.*

JACKFIELD.

THIS Shropshire village, a habitat of potters since the middle of the 16th century, is credited with the production of a somewhat decorative ware, of red body, and extremely brilliant black glaze, adorned with embossed ornament, and frequently with oil-gilding. The piece we illustrate, No. 671, Coll. J.E.H., nearly corresponds in date with what is believed to have been the commencement of the manufacture of this particular ware. Dated pieces are rare, but many of the surviving specimens now presenting an undecorated surface may have been originally inscribed, the oil-gilding rapidly disappearing under frequent ablutions.

1760. (No. 671.) A Two-handled Posset-Pot, decorated in oil-gilding with birds and flowers. Inscribed with initials and date—

M 1760 H

Height 6½ *in.; diameter* 6½ *in.*

COLL. *J.E.H.*

1766. (No. 672.) Two large Tea-Pots, bearing inscription and date—

IAM + GIBLET 1766   IAM + HARE 1766

COLL. *L. MUS.*

1767. (No. 673.) A Jug; decorated in oil-gilding, and inscribed with initials and date—

M H 1767.

Height 6¼ *in.*

1769. (No. 674.) A Jug; decorated in oil-gilding, and inscribed in front, below the spout, with names and date—

Blyth & Elizabeth
Simpson . Derby
1769

Height 9 *in.; diameter* 4½ *in.* COLL. *J.H.*

1781. (No. 675.) A Two-handled Vase or Drinking-Cup; decorated with bird and flowers in oil-gilding—

T S 1781.

Height 6½ *in.; diameter* 7½ *in.* COLL. *A.E.C.*

JACKFIELD, UNDATED.

(No. 676.) A large Tea-Pot; inscribed in oil-gilding—

Mrs Eliz. Roufe.

Height 7 *in.; diameter* 6¼ *in.* COLL. *J.E.H.*

(No. 677.) A Jug; decorated with scroll ornamentation in oil-gilding, and inscribed with motto—

May the tenant be ready when the steward comes

SWINTON.

THE pottery produced at Swinton seems at first to have been a salt-glazed ware, almost identical with that of Nottingham, and an example of this is to be found at No. 678; but white, brown, and yellow earthenware were afterwards made at the same works, where also, towards the end of the last century, the well-known Rockingham ware, with its brilliant chocolate-coloured glaze, was extensively manufactured.

1759. (No. 678.) A Posset-Pot, with two handles, and incised floral decoration. (The ware at this period seems greatly to have resembled that of Nottingham.) Inscribed with date. This interesting example has a fragment of a label, written at "Swinton Pottery," which authenticates it as having been made by or for John Brameld. Mentioned by Mr. Jewitt.

1773. (No. 679.) A Tea-Pot; inscribed with name and date. Mentioned by Mr. Jewitt.

Amelia Hallam

1773.

1788. (No. 680.) A Two-handled Drinking-Cup, of fine white earthenware, with a bluish-coloured glaze; some parts ornamented with blue transfer printing, and the rest of the vessel black, with the name, date, and ornaments in gold. The printed borders are much the same as those around "willow-pattern" plates. Mentioned by Mr. Jewitt.

William Brameld. 1788.

1795. (No. 681.) A Double-handled Drinking-Cup; inscribed with name and date. Mentioned by Mr. Jewitt.

JOHN ALESBROOK

1795.

FAREHAM(?)

THE designation of Fareham, from a village in Hampshire, is the denomination given by some collectors to the very quaint ware of which specimens are given—Nos. 682, 683, and 685. We confess that, although it satisfies on all grounds our requirements as to date and character, we can offer no information as to its real origin. It cannot be ranked as "Slip" ware, the shapes of which it affects, as the ornament is not trickled on to the surface, but *appliqué;* and the examples are too few in number to afford much enlightenment.

1706. (No. 682.) A Posset-Pot, with Eight Handles; dull brownish glaze, decorated in dull green and lighter brown. Inscribed with initials, day of the month, date, and a portion of the alphabet, the letters being in high and sharp relief, and their surface roughened with V-shaped lines.

MAY·THE·27·DAY·
IW· 1706
A BCDEFG HILK AK

Height 8 *in.; diameter* $7\frac{1}{4}$ *in.*

B. Mus. (*Willett Coll.*).

1711. (No. 683). A Posset-Pot, with Eight Handles and Cover; surmounted with a crown. This is a quaint piece, and has many characteristics in common with the preceding, but we are not fully convinced of its authenticity.

ZARAH·OATLY·
HVR·BOOL·1711
BOO·BR·AF·BOO·
YZ·DR·OH·YO·

Height $6\frac{3}{4}$ *in.*

COLL. LATE *W.E.*

1760. (No. 684.) A Dish; decorated with a bird on a branch, and inscribed with date.

(No. 685.) A Circular Dish, of red ware; decorated in brown and yellow, heightened with green, with the figures of Adam and Eve, each holding a stick with a round fan attached to the end, in the stead of the usual fig-leaf. Inscribed with initials, but no date.

G. S.T. M. S.T.

Diameter 12 *in.*

COLL. LATE *W.E.*

NOTES.

(No. 106.) A Three-handled Posset-Pot. Slip-decorated.

This Posset-Pot was discovered, in the the year 1863, by Mr. Albert Hartshorne, of Bradbourne Hall, Wirksworth, Derby, in a very small inn at the foot of the hill on the north side of Dodford Church, near Wieldon, Northamptonshire, and a sketch made of it and full particulars noted at the time. Since then both Inn and Pot have completely vanished, and no trace of either, as far as we can discover, is to be found. It is an interesting piece, being of an early date and bearing the name of a well-known family of potters of that period, though it may have been made by a relation—John Mier—of whose handiwork the two preceding specimens in our list bear authentic record.

(No. 136.) A Nest of Six Cups; now under "Slip-decorated."

This specimen should have appeared on page 62, under the heading of Sgrafiato, to which ware it belongs; but having been attributed by its late owner to Slip-ware, the mistake was not discovered until after his death, when the pages were already finished and the alteration impossible.

(No. 207.) A Plate, Sgrafiato. Coll. Dr. Norris.

(No. 404.) A Plate, Lambeth Delft. Coll. John Eliot Hodgkin.

We are indebted to Dr. Norris, of South Petherton, co. Somerset, for the following information:—

On the 19th May, 1680, O.S., at Ile Brewers, near Langport, in the County of Somerset, there was born a double child, or rather two perfect female children united by a fold of skin or membrane down one side of each. This monstrous birth excited at the time a large amount of interest, which was made apparent in various ways. The parish registers of Ile Brewers during the 17th century have, unfortunately, been lost or destroyed; but there is contemporary evidence of the truth of the occurrence. The Rev. Andrew Paschall, who was inducted to the living of Chedzoy, Somerset, on the extrusion of Mr. Henry Jeanes, under the Black Bartholomew's Act, in 1662, and who was considered to be a very learned man, but who partook of the prevalent superstitious tendencies of the day, considered it an omen of impending evil. Shortly before the invasion of the Duke of Monmouth, he wrote in haste to a person in an eminent station to represent to the King his apprehensions, and to entreat him to cast an eye that way. Amongst other portents he particularises this Ile Brewers event, in the following terms:—"Before our troubles came on, we had some "such signs as used to be deemed forerunners of such things. In May, 1680, here was "that monstrous birth at Ile Brewers, a parish in Somerset, which at that time was taken "much notice of, two female children joined in their bodies from the breast downwards. "They were born May the 19th, and christened by the names of Aquila and Priscilla. "May the 29th I saw them well and likely to live," etc. etc. The identity of the two

"Parsons" (= persons) who robbed the parents to keep the child is well established, one of them being Capt. Henry Walrond, J.P., of Walrond Park, Ile Brewers, County Somerset, "a persecuting Justice of the Peace so-called, though one of the greatest "disturbers of it;" the other being Sir Edward Phillips (or Phelips), Knight, of Montacute, County Somerset, also a great harrier of the Quakers. We are indebted to John Whiting, the Long Sutton Quaker, for a relation of the sad results of the rapacity and cruelty of these two worthies. ("Persecution Exposed." London, 1715.) Speaking of Capt. Walrond, he remarks :—"I cannot but add a few words concerning him and his "end. He dwelt at Elbaiers, about ten miles westward of Ivelchester; a comely, proper "man; had a fair estate, a fine house and park; but after he took up this work of "persecution (being made a Justice in 1670, as a fit tool to put the Conventicle Act "in execution), nothing prospered with him. . . . . He kept the gang of brooms "aforesaid about him, who helped to devour his estate as they had done others, several "of whom came to sad ends; and, to recover his sinking state, he and Sir E—— P—— "took away a twin child, or children (that grew together), from a poor woman to make "a show of them for money, and kept them till they died, to their great shame and "dishonour in the country, for which they were prosecuted in the Crown Office; but "might, I suppose, overcame right." Whiting goes on to say that when Walrond was summoned to appear, he kept his bed, "faining himself sick," rather than do so. Meantime he was presented to the King by a great man at Court as "one of his best "subjects in all the West of England," in commendation of his persecutions. Yet, "I "say it did not at all make him rich but rather the poorer; for he became so poor "that 'twas reported he could not be trusted for a sixpenny loaf, and that he did spin "for his living before he died. And his house dropt through ready to fall about his "ears, and rotted a good chest of Linnen of great value, and at last died miserable poor, "as well as miserable otherwise, and after his death was said to walk at noonday" (a legend it may be noted that has not yet died out in the immediate neighbourhood). The word *broom* is evidently a punning allusion to the family of that name, one of whom married Walrond's daughter. They are elsewhere described as parasites of that gentleman, contributing largely to his unhappy end. Whiting speaks of them as Walrond's "assistants, whose names were Brooms (who used to sweep all away)."

(No. 278.) A Posset-Pot, Lambeth Delft. Coll. J. E. H.

This interesting piece of Lambeth Delft, which bears the initials of a name well known in our own time, was purchased some years ago for Mr. Edkins at the sale of the effects of a gentleman, a descendant of and bearing the same name as the ancestor for whom it was made in the year 1651. At the sale of the late Mr. Edkins' collection it passed into the hands of its present possessor.

FINIS.